Companion to t

6. Worshipping God Together

Michael J. Townsend

Companion to the Lectionary

6. Worshipping God Together

EPWORTH PRESS

0 7162 0503 3

*First Published 1996
by Epworth Press
1 Central Buildings Westminster
London SW1H 9NH*

*Typeset by Regent Typesetting, London
Printed and bound in Great Britain by
Biddles Ltd, Guildford and King's Lynn*

Contents

Contributors

Martyn D. Atkins
Kenneth C. Carveley
Neil Dixon
Julie Hulme
Judith Lampard
John E. Minor
Christine Odell
Jan Sutch Pickard
Peter Sheasby
Michael J. Townsend
Margaret Wallwork
Norman Wallwork

Preface

Volume 5 of the Epworth Companion to the Lectionary Series, *All Together for Worship*, has been widely used and appreciated. When, despite some uncertainties about which lectionary the major churches would work with in the final years of the decade, it became evident to the Epworth Editorial Committee that a similar collection, covering years A and B of JLG2 would be useful, I willingly responded to the challenge of editing such a volume.

A relatively large team of experienced writers was required if the work was to be completed in time for publication to take place before Year A came round again. All those who were invited to take part responded positively, and I am more grateful than I can say to my fellow contributors for the work they have done. Almost without exception their material was sent to me on time, even though all of them lead very busy lives. It is a particular pleasure that one of our contributors, Jan Sutch Pickard, will become the Vice President of the Methodist Conference at about the time this book is published. A special word of gratitude is due to Peter Sheasby who edited Volume 5. He not only agreed to contribute to this one, but freely shared with me his editorial experience from the previous volume and thus saved me from several pitfalls!

Users of this book will quickly discern that a variety of styles may be found within it. Although contributors wrote to fairly strict guidelines in regard to such matters as format and length, each has produced material in her or his own distinctive manner, and no attempt has been made to impose editorial uniformity. We do however, have a common hope and prayer that what we have written may prove useful to those who lead all-age worship.

Leeds, August 1995   Michael J. Townsend

Introduction

For most of Christian history all-age worship has needed no defence. It is the way in which the vast majority of Christians have always worshipped. Even today, Orthodox and Catholic Christians worship in this way as a matter of course, and find it difficult to see why others should make such a fuss about it. In these traditions children and young people participate in the church's liturgy from a very early age. Through their participation they learn to answer for themselves the question, 'What do you mean by this observance' (Ex. 12.26). The problem, if problem it is, mainly affects Protestant churches.

The rise of the Sunday School movement in the eighteenth century led to children being removed from the main act of worship, in order to be taken elsewhere for instruction and worship of a kind considered more suitable for them. There was much to be said for this development, especially given the uncompromisingly word-centred nature of most Protestant worship at that time, and Sunday Schools did much good work. There were, however, losses as well as gains. When adults habitually worship without children being present the mistaken notion that Christian worship is an essentially cerebral activity is reinforced. This can lead to a situation where creativity and imagination, the use of symbols and colours, drama, dance, mime and the like, are thought of as being 'for the children' and worship is thus impoverished. Quite simply, the people of God need one another in worship if what is offered to God is to be both worthy and enriching. From the children's point of view, it can be extremely difficult to make the transition from Sunday School to a strange 'adult' activity known as worship, when attendance at Sunday School comes to an end. There can be few churches which have not agonized over the large numbers of young people who are lost to the life of the church at that point.

The move towards all-age worship is, at least in part, an attempt to find solutions to these problems, to experience what it means to worship together as the people of God, and to enable children to feel at home in worship from an early age. There are some churches, not many, where every Sunday morning is all-age worship throughout. Many more churches have all-age worship once a month or on special occasions in the life of the church. In almost every church which has a Sunday School or Junior Church, the children are present for part of the worship. Usually this means they form part of the congregation for the first ten or fifteen minutes and then leave for their own activities. Sometimes, perhaps more imaginatively, they have their own worship and learning first, and join the adults after the 'Ministry of the Word' when something of what they have been doing in Junior Church can be shared with the whole congregation and all can be gathered up in thanksgiving, intercession and Holy Communion. In either case, a significant part of the Sunday morning worship needs to be an all-age occasion.

It is a great temptation to regard that part of the worship for which children are present *not* as all-age, but as 'the children's bit'. This unhelpful idea is reinforced if it is the custom for the Sunday School (which usually in practice means one of the teachers) to choose 'the children's hymn' and a children's address is delivered before they leave. Under those circumstances it is quite difficult for the adults to avoid thinking, as the children depart, that 'their' worship is about to begin. It is, of course, much easier to lead ten minutes of children's worship than it is to lead ten minutes of genuine all-age worship, but when we yield to that temptation we miss the mutual enrichment which comes from the whole family of God worshipping together. *Let the People Worship*, the report of the Commission on Worship to the 1988 Methodist Conference defined all-age worship thus: 'Such worship is not primarily designed for one particular age group, neither children nor older people, but rather seeks to lead the people together into thanksgiving, praise or adoration. In such services, whether termed all-age, family or parade, the presence of children can enhance the worship for older people and the presence of older people can enhance the worship for children.' This then, is the challenge which faces those who lead all-age worship in our churches.

All Christian worship is a response to God's gracious love shown to us in Jesus Christ. In all-age worship this response should be expressed in ways which can be owned and used by those who are present. It needs to be emphasized that this should not mean a watering-down of the great themes of Christian faith. Children, just as much as adults, need to offer praise and adoration to God for his mighty acts in Christ, to know what it is to be forgiven and accepted, to experience grace and the presence of the Holy Spirit and to be given the opportunity to commit themselves, through worship, to the service of God and other people. Children, just as much as adults, need to know how the Christian faith helps us to deal with the great issues of human life such as guilt and suffering, and to understand something of the cost of discipleship. Such things must not be ignored in all-age worship, rather they need to be explored in ways which are appropriate and helpful. Nor should it be supposed that in order for this to be done, language and imagery must be over-simplified. Children often have a creative if untutored response to the central images of the Christian story, and it is our task in worship to nurture that response. The prayers which are provided in this book are therefore *not* children's prayers; they are prayers for use when, for all or part of a service, the whole community of faith is worshipping God together.

Worship leaders and preachers must feel quite free to make use of the material in this book in whatever way they find helpful. It will sometimes be appropriate to use prayers as they stand; on other occasions they will need to be adapted. The material is based on years A and B of the JLG2 Lectionary, but with use of the indexes could be utilized by those who use the ASB (JLG1), Revised Common Lectionary, or no lectionary at all.

Each set of prayers begins with either a **Theme** or a **Presentation**. The former offers brief reflections on the topic; the latter also includes practical suggestions about how to present it. There usually follows a **Call to Worship**, and then a range of prayers for use at various points in the worship. Comments on Volume 5 suggest that prayers at the **Offering** have been particularly appreciated, and we have therefore included them whenever possible. The material usually concludes with a **Dismissal**, to which, in almost all cases, a Trinitarian blessing can appropriately be added.

How to use this book

As a rule:

- words in Roman type are to be said
- words in *italic* are instructions or, occasionally, quotations
- words in **bold** type are for congregational participation.

Responses within prayers can be simply introduced or printed on the church noticesheet. There are some prayers where the words are not a straightforward repetition of a phrase and in such cases the whole prayer can be copied (for single occasion use, see copyright note at the front of the book). If this is not possible or desired, either two voices can be used or the whole prayer read by the worship leader alone.

Material for Year A

9th Sunday before Christmas

Prov. 8.1, 22–31
Rev. 21.1–4, 22–27
Matt. 10.28–33

Presentation

Taken together the readings suggest the difficult but worthwhile theme of God's eternal existence. Consider images which take us progressively backwards to 'before all things' and forwards to 'after all things'. Focus upon God's creativity, care and compassion. The Gospel reminds us that eternity includes the 'now' which is vital but should not be dominant.

Prayer of Adoration

Eternal God, Father, Son and Holy Spirit,
we worship you.

You existed before the universe began.
You designed the world, and brought into being all you planned.

We spoiled your design.
We failed you and rejected you.
Yet instead of rejecting us you gave yourself for us,
dying on a cross, demonstrating how much we mean to you.

You will be there after the world has ended,
making new heavens,
living with your people,
and all sadness and death will be gone.

From first to last, from beginning to end, you are God,
and we love and adore you.   **Amen**

Prayer of Intercession

God of never-failing compassion
we pray for those who cannot forget the past
  who are burdened by dark things they have done
  who wish they could live their lives over again.
Lord, come among them,
Be their Light and hope.

We pray for those who need you today
   the poor and the rich ...
   the old and the young ...
   the sick and the healthy ...
   the living and the dying ...
Lord, come among them,
Be their Light and hope.

We pray for those who fear the future,
   those who have no faith in you,
   those who are without any hope.
Lord, come among them,
Be their Light and hope.   Amen

Prayer of Dedication (*Based on a prayer by Alcuin, 735–804*)

Eternal Light, shine into our lives,
Eternal Goodness, guard us from evil,
Eternal Power, be our strength,
Eternal Wisdom, guide our thinking,
Eternal love, inspire our living
   that in all we think and say and do
   we may reflect your nature;
   through Jesus Christ our Lord.   **Amen**

Blessing

Go in peace:
may the Wisdom of God fill you,
the Light of God thrill you,
and the Power of God will you
towards better discipleship of Jesus:
and may the blessing of God,
the Father, the Son, and the Holy Spirit,
be with you throughout eternity.   **Amen**

8th Sunday before Christmas

Presentation

It is symptomatic of the Fall that human beings constantly try to replace the one true God with other 'gods', whether it be with idols, as in Isaiah, or with proud hypocrisy, as in Matthew. God's remedy is declared in Romans. The focus should be upon our false 'gods', the one true God, and the remedy. Various types of 'other gods' can be on display and could be symbolically done away with at some point.

Call to Worship

'God has demonstrated his love for us
in that while we were still sinners Christ died for us.'
Let us worship the Lord.

Prayer of Adoration

God of patience and mercy,
we praise you for your forgiving love;
in our darkness you are the one true light,
in our sin you are the one true hope.
Though we are unworthy, we worship you as we are able,
through Jesus Christ our Lord. **Amen**

Litany of Confession *With an assurance of pardon*

Let us pray to God, admitting our faults and asking for forgiveness.
Gracious and Holy God:
    When we love our possessions and money more than you
    Forgive us.
    When we turn the talents and gifts you have given us into idols
    Forgive us.
    When we put things before people
    Forgive us.
    When we spend all our time and resources on ourselves
    Forgive us.
    When we speak and act as if You are not our God
    Forgive us. *Silence*
It is God's nature to forgive those who are truly sorry.

The One True God never despairs of our fickle human nature,
The One True God is always ready to help us begin again.
So hear the word of pardon:
    Through God in Jesus Christ, your sins are forgiven.   **Amen**

Meditation   *On the Gospel*

How lovely it looked. Bright orange, promising juice and zest.
I picked it specially, cut it open with anticipation – mouth-watering.
It was as dry as a bone – and full of pips!
Flattering to deceive. A real orange but … not truly an orange at all!
How lovely it looked. Bright orange, promising juice and zest.
But looks can be deceiving.

Prayer for Illumination   *Before the sermon*

O True and Living God,
open our deaf ears, and give sight to our blind eyes,
that we may receive your word, and perceive your purposes,
through Jesus Christ our Lord.   **Amen**

Prayer of Dedication

Lord Jesus Christ,
whose words and actions united
to declare the saving grace of God,
Work in us, we pray,
that our lives and lips may agree with each other
and bring glory to our Father in Heaven.   **Amen**

Gen. 13.1–18
Gal. 3.1–14
Matt. 3.7–12

7th Sunday before Christmas

Presentation

*References to Abraham connect these passages, but the key theme is a life lived believing – demonstrating faith in – **the promises of God**, and God's faithfulness to those promises. Can occasions of broken promises, and promises kept, be shared? Can occasions when what seemed unbelievable actually happened?*

Call to worship

God's promises are for you, for your children,
and for all who are far away, everyone whom the Lord our God
calls.
Let us worship God.

Prayer of Confession

Forgive us, Lord,
    when we ask you to guide us,
    but we choose the way we want to go;
    when we ask you to fulfil your promises
    but we are not prepared to meet your demands;
    when we ask for your forgiveness,
    but we don't believe that you have forgiven us.
Forgive us, Lord, and increase our faith in you.   **Amen**

Prayer of Thanksgiving

Faithful God,
utterly to be trusted,
we thank you for your generous promises;
    for grace exceeding our expectations and our deserving.
We thank you for the example of great men and women;
    for those whose trust in you declares your faithfulness.
We thank you for Jesus Christ:
    who by his words and example,
    his obedience to your will,
    his dying and rising from death,
    declared to every person on earth your eternal promises.

We thank you for the Holy Spirit
  who prepares the way for faith, and is the proof of it.
Wonderful God, Father, Son and Holy Spirit,
receive our thanks and praise.   **Amen**

Prayer of Intercession

God promised a land to Abraham and his descendants:
  Let us pray
  For those who are at war over areas of land,
  and those who suffer because of it ...
  L: Lord, have mercy: R: **Lord, have mercy.**

For refugees who have been forced to leave their homeland
and have nothing to call their own ...
L: Lord, have mercy: R: **Lord, have mercy.**

For those whose land produces nothing, and they go hungry ...
L: Lord, have mercy: R: **Lord, have mercy.**

For victims of earthquakes, floods and natural disasters ...
L: Lord, have mercy: R: **Lord, have mercy.**

For those who poison the planet and pollute the earth, who have
no thought for the generations yet to come ...
L: Lord, have mercy: R: **Lord, have mercy.   Amen**

Prayer of Dedication

Faithful God,
may what we have heard with our ears and said with our lips
be believed in our hearts;
and may what is believed in our hearts be seen in our lives,
to the praise of Jesus Christ our Lord.   **Amen**

6th Sunday before Christmas

Presentation

Doing the will of God *is the overall theme. Matthew and Acts both suggest the actions and behaviour required of anyone wanting to do God's will. Photographs of people 'who do/have done the will of God' can be displayed. 'Why' and 'how' they do God's will should be made clear.*

Call to Worship

The promises of God through the prophets are ours,
we rejoice as we worship the Lord.

Prayer of Adoration

Wonderful God, Father, Son and Holy Spirit:
   whose thoughts are higher than our thoughts,
   whose words are deeper than our words,
   whose purposes are broader than ours,
   whose mercy is wider than ours;
   yet who never ceases to make known
   your thoughts and words, your purposes and mercy to people like us,
   we worship and adore your holy name.   **Amen**

Act of Confession (*Based on the Gospel passage, and could be used as a response to God's Word*)

Lord Jesus, forgive us
   when we fail to follow your teaching and example.
   When we have taken revenge and retaliated
   instead of offering the other cheek:
L: Lord, forgive us: R: **Lord, forgive us.**

   When we have begrudged giving small things
   instead of offering more than was asked:
L: Lord, forgive us: R: **Lord, forgive us.**

When we have resented going out of our way for people
instead of cheerfully going the extra mile:
L: Lord, forgive us: R: **Lord, forgive us.**

When we have flatly refused to do what was asked of us
even when we knew you wanted us to do it:
L: Lord, forgive us: R: **Lord, forgive us.**

When we have not loved our enemies,
or prayed for those who persecute us:
L: Lord, forgive us: R: **Lord, forgive us.**

Give us strength Lord,
to do what you ask and to follow your example,
for we long to do your will.   **Amen**

Thanksgiving

Eternal God,
We thank you for prophets who delivered your word and declared
your will.
We thank you for Jesus, the greatest of prophets,
your Living Word, and your perfect will.
We thank you for the Holy Spirit
who strengthens us to proclaim your word and do your will.
All praise and thanks be to you for ever and ever.   **Amen**

Some Suggested Themes for Intercession

Let us pray for those who seek to do God's will
For those who serve others in need …
For those who speak out against injustice …
For those who declare your love and truth through word and
deed…
For all ministers, evangelists and those in Christian mission work…
For those who are finding it hard to obey God …
For those who cannot do what they would like to do for God …

Dismissal

Go in God's power, and with God's blessing
for in that alone is your hope and salvation.   **Amen**

5th Sunday before Christmas

Presentation

*The theme of **Jesus the Just Judge** dominates the Epistle and Gospel. Images of lawcourts, justice, and judges will be useful, but the righteousness of God's judgment must not be eclipsed. Revelation requires drama and gravity. Matthew's 'sheep and goats' are ripe for dramatic productions, but care must be taken not to reduce this devastating text to mere comedy.*

⅄ Litany of praise and adoration

Just and compassionate God –
faithful and true
We worship you.

Protector of your people
We worship you.

Shepherd of your sheep
We worship you.

Word of God
We worship you.

King of kings and Lord of lords
We worship you.   **Amen**

Act of Confession

Forgive us Lord, that we live in a world where so often
   the starving go unfed,
   the thirsty remain parched,
   and strangers are not befriended.
L: Lord, have mercy: R: **Lord, have mercy.**

Forgive us Lord that we live in communities where so often
   the sick go untended,
   the naked remain exposed,
   and prisoners are not visited.
L: Christ, have mercy: R: **Christ, have mercy**.

Forgive us Lord, that so often we are content that it be so.
  Lord, have mercy.
  Lord, have mercy.

You are a warrior for justice, and we quake before your fierce
anger. You are faithful and true, and we throw ourselves upon your
mercy, it is our only hope, but it is enough.   **Amen**

Prayer of Intercession (*Several voices can be used here.*)

King of kings
we pray for the leaders of communities and nations ...

Lord of lords
we pray for those trapped by false faiths and manipulative
leaders ...

Protector of your people
we pray for the poor ... the oppressed ... the imprisoned ...

Word of God
we pray for the church ... for its mission and members ...

Faithful and True One
we pray for the broken hearted ... the faithless ... the confused ...
In the name of Christ.   **Amen**

Prayer of Dedication

Just and Holy God,
work in our lives by the power of your Spirit,
so that love of you, not fear of judgment
may stir us to act justly and with compassion;
that when we meet you face to face,
we may rejoice in your eternal presence:
through Jesus Christ our Lord.   **Amen**

4th Sunday before Christmas
Advent 1

Presentation

Be Prepared *is the theme. Preparations of various sorts could be made: e.g. how do we prepare for a guest? How do you get ready for unexpected events? The 'Dramatized Bible' has good versions of all three lessons.*

Advent Litany

O Lord of Lords, come and save us.
Amen. Come, Lord Jesus.

O Root of Jesse, delay no longer.
Amen. Come, Lord Jesus.

O Key of David, unlock the door to heaven.
Amen. Come, Lord Jesus.

O Emmanuel, reveal God's glory to us.
Amen. Come, Lord Jesus.

O come Lord Jesus, raise us to the joy of your kingdom.
Amen. Come, Lord Jesus.

Prayer of Confession

Merciful God,
Though we are not perfect, may we be forgiven,
though we are not stunningly effective, may we be faithful,
though we are not holy, may we press on in faith,
though we are undeserving, may we be accepted by you;
through Jesus Christ our Lord.   **Amen**

An Honest Advent Prayer?

Don't you dare come now, Lord!
We're not expecting you. We're not ready yet.
Besides, it isn't Christmas for weeks.

That's when you're expected. That's when we'll be ready,
And not before.
You can come to us then. By then we'll be delighted to see you.
By then all will be prepared: tinsel and turkey for a baby in a
manger, soft, inoffensive, wide-eyed. That's the Jesus we're
expecting.
We'll be devastated if you jump the gun.
So please, you won't be coming before Christmas … will you?

Prayer of Intercession

Everlasting peace:
Soon, Lord, soon.

Nations walking in your way:
Soon, Lord, soon.

Disputes settled according to your will:
Soon, Lord, soon.

Swords becoming ploughs:
Soon, Lord, soon.

Neighbours caring for each other as for themselves:
Soon, Lord, soon.

Your will being done on earth as it is in heaven:
Soon, Lord, soon.   Amen

Prayer of Dedication

Prepare us for your coming, Lord.
help us to use our time wisely, reject all that displeases you,
and love our neighbours as we love ourselves.
Strengthen our discipleship, so that when Jesus comes,
we may rejoice to be with him for ever.   **Amen**

Dismissal

May the God of everlasting peace make you holy in all things
that you may be ready at the coming of our Lord Jesus
Christ.   **Amen**

3rd Sunday before Christmas
Advent 2

Presentation

God's desire to right wrongs *takes precedence over 'Bible Sunday'.*
Produce several things which are not as they should be: e.g. a clock,
a broken arm!, a scene of war or hunger, etc. How can these be put
right? Some are easy, others difficult. Sometimes we can do it
ourselves, sometimes others have to do it for us. The key aim is to
declare that God wants to right wrongs, and it is crucial the balance
is struck between the 'without God, we cannot' and 'without us, God
will not' principles.

Prayer of Confession
Closely based upon the passage from Isaiah, and might be used
after it

Lord, what a sinful race we are!
We rebel against you, we oppress others, and dishonour ourselves.
Our thoughts are false, our words are lies, and our deeds are empty.
You are not pleased with us; with what we think and say and do.
Pause
In spite of all this you love us!
You want to put things right, and we want that too.
Come to us like a rushing river cleansing our sin,
washing away our selfishness.
Come to us like a strong wind whipping us into holy action,
filling your world with the breath of life,
through Jesus Christ our Lord.   **Amen**

Prayer of Intercession

Let us pray to God
    who longs to bring justice and healing to the world, saying
    Lord, through your power and your people:
    Set wrongs right.

    Wherever there is injustice and abuse of power ...
    Lord, through your power and your people:
    Set wrongs right.

Wherever there is hunger, poverty and the disease they cause …
Lord, through your power and your people:
Set wrongs right.

Wherever your gifts are squandered and abused …
Lord, through your power and your people:
Set wrongs right.

Wherever your church does not do your will
Lord, through your power and your people:
Set wrongs right.

Wherever people are needlessly damaged and hurting
Lord, through your power and your people:
Set wrongs right.

Give to us, O Lord, your own power,
that our desire to set wrongs right might be made clear in actions
which are true to your holy will:
through Jesus Christ our Lord.   **Amen**

Prayer of dedication

Just and holy God,
Help us to hate sin like you do;
love sinners like you do;
help the oppressed like you do;
desire to set things right like you do.   **Amen**

Offering

Receive, Lord, what we freely offer to you, and help us to freely
offer to others what we have received from you.   **Amen**

Dismissal

The Day of the Lord is surely coming.
Be fervent in the work of God's kingdom.
Amen. Come, Lord Jesus.

2nd Sunday before Christmas
Advent 3

Judg. 13.2–14
Phil. 4.4–9
Matt. 11.2–19

Presentation

Anticipation is the theme for today. Not just of John the Baptist who, though important is presented in the Gospel as clearly inferior to Jesus. The Epistle hits the mark: The Lord is near, it is **his** coming we anticipate. Pictures of road signs which indicate what is ahead may be useful, and draw attention the right response: slowing down for a sharp bend, low gear for a steep hill, etc. How do we respond to the news that Jesus is near?

Call to Worship

The Lord is near. The Lord is coming soon.
Rejoice in the Lord always. Again I say, Rejoice.

Litany of Adoration

God of creation and covenant:
We praise and adore you.

God of prophecy and promises:
We praise and adore you.

God of holiness and healing:
We praise and adore you.

Through Jesus Christ our Lord.   **Amen**

Prayer of Confession

Lord forgive us,
when we are not obedient to your will;
when we are reluctant to pray;
when we think about what is untrue and unlovely;
when we are deaf to your voice,
and blind to the signs of your coming to us;
when we live as if we are not expecting you.

Lord forgive us and fill us with anticipation of your coming to
reign.   **Amen**

Prayer of Intercession

St Paul wrote: 'The Lord is near. Do not be anxious about anything
but by prayer make your requests known to God.' So we pray,
For those with no hope,
those filled with anxiety,
and those who cannot pray.
L: Lord: R: **Let them know you are near.**

For those whose minds are twisted,
those filled with hatred,
and those who cannot love anyone.
L: Lord: R: **Let them know you are near.**

For those who are deaf and blind,
those filled with scepticism,
those who cannot believe in you.
L: Lord: R: **Let them know you are near.**

For those we *are* anxious about
but who in faith we lift to you in prayer …
L: Lord: R: **Let them know you are near.   Amen**

Prayer of Dedication

Give to us, Lord,
ears to hear what you are saying;
eyes to see what you are doing;
strength to be obedient to your will;
courage to declare what we know is true;
and the desire to prepare for your coming
through Jesus Christ our Lord.   **Amen**

Dismissal

May the peace of God and the God of peace be with
you all.   **Amen**

Sunday next before Christmas
Advent 4

Presentation

The theme is 'God is with us'. Clearly the 'Virgin' in Isaiah, the 'Woman' in Revelation, and Mary in Matthew are linked, and should be prominent but not dominant today. That God comes in Jesus should be dominant. Explore the significance of names: what does their Christian name mean? Why the same surname as parents? etc. Jesus' name is 'Immanuel'.

Call to Worship

Heaven is opened. A virgin gives birth to a son.
His name is Immanuel, and God is with us. Let us worship God.

Prayer of Adoration

O God who created the heavens and the earth;
who opened the gates of heaven
and came in Christ to save all things:
We adore your holy name.

O God who made a covenant with your people,
who sent prophets to declare your will
and came in Christ to save all people:
We adore your holy name.

O God who prepared a way of salvation,
who chose obedient servants like Mary and Joseph
and came in Christ to save each one of us:
We adore your holy name.   Amen

Prayer of Confession

Forgive us, Lord,
When we demand signs and wonders before we will trust in you;
when we are not obedient to your will,
and find endless excuses for what we say and do;

when we do not appreciate who Jesus is, and what he has done for us;
Lord, forgive us.   **Amen**

Prayer of Intercession

Let us pray:
Son of Mary, we pray for all families
especially those who are coping with changes in their lives
together ... (moving house, school, new baby, someone in
hospital, divorce etc.)
L: Immanuel: God is with us: R: **Be with them, we pray.**

Son of David, we pray for all the nations of the world,
especially those which are at war, or suffering some disaster ...
L: Immanuel: God is with us: R: **Be with them, we pray.**

Son of Man, we pray for all the people we know,
especially those who are sad at this time of joy ...
L: Immanuel: God is with us: R: **Be with them, we pray.**

Son of God, we pray for those who have no hope or faith ...
especially those who are dreading this Christmastime ...
L: Immanuel: God is with us: R: **Be with them, we pray.**
Amen

Offering Prayer

Almighty God,
as Mary rejoiced to be your humble servant,
and Joseph was content to do your will,
receive these gifts we offer,
as symbols that we too desire to be your servants
and seek to do your will, through Jesus Christ our Lord.   **Amen**

Dismissal

Go to share the good news of Christ's coming
and may Jesus who is 'Immanuel' be with you always.

Isa. 9.2, 6–7
I John 4.7–14
John 1.1–14

Christmas Day

Presentation

The birth of Christ is pictured chiefly in terms of God's Light coming into the world, so the theme is **God's Son – the light of the world.** *Talk about (and display?) different sorts of light and its uses: e.g. torches, lighthouses; the Sun; etc. The point is to declare what it means to say Jesus comes as the Light. Isaiah and John would repay being read by several voices.*

Litany of Praise

Let us praise the Lord
The Word made flesh has come among us! God is with us.
Alleluia!
The Light of God illuminates the world! God is with us.
Alleluia!
The Saviour comes to set us free! God is with us.
Alleluia!
Christ is born of Mary! God is with us.
Alleluia!
His name is Immanuel! God is with us.
Alleluia!
The Prince of Peace shall reign forever! God is with us.
Alleluia!

Prayer of Confession

Forgive us, Lord.
You send your Eternal Light into the world,
but so often we choose to remain in darkness.
L: Lord, have mercy: R: **Lord, have mercy.**

Forgive us, Lord.
You show your love for us by sending your Son into the world;
but so often we do not love one another.
L: Christ, have mercy: R: **Christ, have mercy.**

Forgive us, Lord.
You offer us the privilege of becoming your children;
but so often we do not recognize or receive Jesus your Son.
L: Lord, have mercy: R: **Lord, have mercy.**

God of love, forgive our sins, and set us free to worship you,
through Jesus Christ our Lord.   **Amen**

Prayer of Intercession

Wonderful Counsellor,
we pray for all who need your wisdom and guidance ...
L: Lord hear us: R: **Lord, graciously hear us.**

Mighty God,
we pray for all who need your strength and support ...
L: Lord hear us: R: **Lord, graciously hear us.**

Everlasting Father,
we pray for all who need your love and justice ...
L: Lord hear us: R: **Lord, graciously hear us.**

Prince of Peace
we pray for all who need your comfort and care ...
L: Lord hear us: R: **Lord, graciously hear us.   Amen**

Dismissal

Go from this place glorifying and praising God:
and may the Wonderful Counsellor guide you,
the Mighty God keep you,
the Everlasting Father protect you,
the Prince of Peace surround you
and the blessing of God, Father, Son and Holy Spirit
fill your lives and thrill your hearts today and always.   **Amen**

1st Sunday after Christmas

Theme

God reveals his glory in Christ to the nations, calling them to worship him.

Call to Worship

Lift up your eyes and see!
All nations and peoples draw near, to worship Christ the Lord.

Prayer of Adoration

God, your glory shines upon us, scattering our darkness
with the joy and radiance of your presence.
You reveal to us your love and mercy
in Jesus Christ your Son,
that through him we may offer you our praise.
To you, Lord God, belongs the worship
of our hearts and minds, the homage of all peoples,
now and for ever, through Christ our Lord.   **Amen**

Prayer of Intercession

This response may be used in this prayer:
L: Lord of the ages: R: **Lead and guide us**.

Let us pray for the world, and for the witness and service of all
God's people.

We pray for all governments and rulers:
   that those who hold political office and exercise
   authority may show purity of intention in their life and work
   and truth and integrity in their dealings and decisions.

We pray for all relations between nations, cultures and faiths:
   that wealth may be more justly shared,
   diversity of cultures more widely valued and appreciated
   and religions more closely related in dialogue and love of truth.

We pray for all in need of the peace which Christ brings:

that all who are at enmity may be reconciled
and all who are ensnared by evil and falsehood
may turn to God's goodness and truth.

Recalling the gifts of the Magi, we ask for grace to offer our gifts
to God:
the gold of our obedience and service,
the incense of our love and prayer,
the myrrh of our faithfulness and care.

We pray for the refreshment and renewal of all who hear the good
news of Christ's coming:
that the bereaved may find comfort and hope;
that those who lack purpose and meaning may find new
direction;
that all in need may know God's presence with them.

Lord God, in your mercy,
you have come to us in Jesus Christ,
that we may draw near to you.
May our prayers accord with your will,
and our lives reflect our prayer,
that your glory may be known in all the earth,
through Jesus Christ our Lord.   **Amen**

Offering Prayer

Wisdom and power, honour and blessing,
are rightly yours eternal God.
To you belong the riches of the earth,
the treasures of all peoples,
the service of our lives,
through Christ our Lord.   **Amen**

Dismissal

May God who guided the wise to Christ, to know his power and
wisdom, lead and guide you on your way.   **Amen**

Jer. 31.15–17
II Cor. 1.3–11
Matt. 2.13–23

2nd Sunday after Christmas

Theme

God fulfils his purpose in Christ. Even through disaster, human sin and suffering, he delivers and saves his people.

Call to Worship

God is our Saviour and mighty deliverer;
the life and hope of all his people. Let us worship him.

Prayer of Confession

This response may be used in this prayer:
L: Lord to you we cry: R: **Have mercy on us.**

Let us confess to God our involvement in the sin of the world and
ask for grace to amend our lives.
God, our creator and redeemer, you call us to seek you that we may
find your mercy and forgiveness.
We have devalued human life by slaughtering the innocent,
oppressing the poor, and ignoring the needy and distressed.
We have misappropriated the goods of others, making them
strangers to their own land, leaving them devoid of hope.
We have idolized what is false, and refused to give you glory,
worshipping the creation instead of the creator.
We have failed to acknowledge your providence and care, among
the commonwealth of nations, and in our own lives.
Lord our God, forgive us our sins, and restore in us your image and
likeness, that our lives may reflect your glory, through Jesus Christ
our Lord.   **Amen**

Prayer of Intercession

This response may be used in this prayer:
L: By the grace of your Spirit: R: **This is our prayer**.

Lord God, send your Holy Spirit to inspire our prayer which we
offer in the name of Christ.
We remember all who have been dispossessed of their rightful

citizenship and homeland, of their homes, of food and clothing, of human dignity and of human rights and freedom; and all who have been exiled by unjust regimes.

Strengthen our hands, that by your grace, through our work and concern, fullness of life and hope for the future may be restored to them.

We remember all who wield great power and authority, that they may serve others beyond self interest, looking to you for guidance and inspiration.

Strengthen our will, that by your grace, through our discernment and understanding, fullness of life and a common sense of care may be restored to them.

We remember all who are passing through a time of trial: those in weakness and ill health, those who are bereaved and grieving and those caught in circumstances they cannot change, through war, human hatred and ill-will.

Strengthen our hearts, that by your grace, through our love and compassion, fullness of life and peace of mind and heart may be restored to them.

Hear Lord, the prayers which you inspire in the hearts of your people. May they be effectual in our lives, and in the lives of those for whom we pray, through Christ our Lord.   **Amen**

Offering Prayer

All that we have is yours, O Lord, our life, our strength, our faith and hope. With these gifts we acknowledge that all things come from your goodness, through Jesus Christ our Lord.   **Amen**

Dismissal

May God, who is the strength and life of his people, guide and sustain you in his service. To him be glory for ever.   **Amen**

I Sam. 16.1–13a
Rom. 6.12–23
Matt. 3.13–17

1st Sunday after Epiphany

Theme

God's call to service comes often quite unexpectedly and sometimes in the most unlikely ways. God knows us and asks for our obedience in our response.

Call to Worship

Christ is the true light, who enlightens everyone who comes into the world.

Prayer of Confession

Let us confess our sins to God:
God in his son Jesus Christ has set us free
and raised us from death to life;
Yet we have not lived in this freedom as his children,
and have resisted his grace at work in us.
Let us turn to God and ask forgiveness.   *Silence*

Lord God, nothing is hidden from you. Others see our outward actions but you alone read our hearts and minds.
You see our motives and intentions, both those we know and those hidden from others and ourselves.
Grant us the grace of your Spirit, that we may not be deceived, nor think our lives are unknown to you.
What is gracious and good in us, confirm;
what is lacking, supply;
what is weak, restore and renew;
what we repent of, forgive.
We ask this through Christ our Lord.   **Amen**

Prayer of Intercession

This response may be used in this prayer:
L: Lord, to whom all needs are known: R: **Listen to our prayer**.

Let us pray to God our Father, through Jesus Christ his Son, in the power of the Holy Spirit.
For all the rulers and leaders of the nations,

that they may serve their people with wisdom and insight;
For the life of the baptized,
    that Christians everwhere may recognize their common unity
    in Christ; that all whom God calls to serve him may be sustained
    by his Spirit.
For all God's people,
    that they may grow in grace, and be a sign of the new life in
    Christ in the world.
For the grace to seek and do what is God's will for us.
God of all, as we offer these prayers to you, enlighten our minds
and purify our hearts.
May it be our desire to do your will and seek your glory alone,
through Jesus Christ our Lord.   **Amen**

Meditation

'The Lord sees not as man sees.'
This is so in the Old Covenant and in the New; Jesus 'knew what
was in a person'. That God sees into the very depths of our being
may be very disconcerting. God reads our motives and intentions,
and that will often be cause for repentance. Yet it is also reason for
hope and trust in him. For God also sees our true desire in those
circumstances when all does not turn out as we would have wished.
'The deeds God loves most are those that he alone has witnessed.'

(Curé d'Ars)

Dismissal

God who has called you to his service make you strong in faith and
love, that by the grace of his Spirit you may do his will, through
Christ our Lord.   **Amen**

2nd Sunday after Epiphany

Theme

*God calls us to love and obey his commands, that we may proclaim
the good news of his kingdom.*

Call to Worship

O taste and see how gracious the Lord is.
Blessed are they who trust in him.

Prayer of Adoration

God, your power we see in creation's awesome forces,
   in changing forms of light and colour;
   all living things move and breathe
      by the breath of your Spirit ...
God, your word we hear in the generations of Israel
   through outspoken prophets;
   all living truth proclaims your holy will
      by the breath of your Spirit ...
God, your grace we prove in the triumphs and tragedies of
humanity,
   in selfless concern and offering;
   all true desires reach toward you
      by the breath of your Spirit ...
God, your love we know in Jesus Christ your Son,
   in his words and works of power,
   in his dying and his rising,
   all in him die to sin and rise to new life
      by the breath of your Spirit ...
God, you call your people of every time and place to worship you;
   may all that we offer be inspired by your grace
      and the breath of your Spirit ...
   for all glory is yours, now and for ever.   **Amen**

Prayers of Intercession

God called the prophets to speak his truth to their generation.
Christ called his disciples to radical obedience in faith and life.
Let us with all God's people offer our prayers for the church and
the world:

Let us pray for all who are called to prophetic witness in the life of
the world:
    acting and speaking for a juster use of the world's resources;
    voicing the cry of the voiceless and the marginalized;
    combating racism and prejudice.

Let us pray for all who are called to prophetic witness in the life of
the church:
    preaching and teaching the faith;
    ministering to the sick and suffering;
    leaving what is familiar to serve the Lord.

And let us pray for ourselves:
that we too may be signs of contradiction according to the gospel;
that we may have grace to hear God's word and to respond in
obedience;
and that the Spirit who has inspired our prayers may enable us to
serve God and those for whom we pray,
in the name of Christ our Lord.   **Amen**

Offering Prayer

Father, may these gifts which we offer, signs of your love for us, be
also signs of our love and service to you. We ask this through
Christ our Lord.   **Amen**

Dismissal

God who has called us in Christ to serve him,
sends us to proclaim the good news of his kingdom.
To him be praise and glory for ever.   **Amen**

3rd Sunday after Epiphany

Theme

The good news of God's kingdom brings light into the world's darkness.

Call to Worship

Christ is the true light of the world. Those who follow him will not walk in darkness but will have the light of life.

Prayer of Confession

Let us seek God's forgiveness of our sins, confessing that, though the light of Christ has come, we have lived in darkness.

Father of all,
we confess to you our weakness:
forgetting your goodness to us, we have remembered the failings of others;
taking your generous love for granted, we have been unmerciful to others;
and by our hasty judgments, we have judged ourselves in your presence.
In your light we see ourselves clearly. Acknowledging our share in the sin of the world, we seek your forgiveness. *Silence*
God of mercy, forgive our sins,
set our hearts and minds free from the mistakes and errors of the past, that in the freedom of your redeeming grace we may live to serve you, through Jesus Christ our Lord. **Amen**

Prayer of Intercession

This response may be used in this prayer:
L: God of goodness and mercy: R: **Listen to our prayer.**

St Paul says: 'I make mention of you in my prayers continually.'
Let us pray for the life of the world and for all God's people:

We pray for those living in darkness and the shadow of death:
  for communities threatened and destroyed by war or

terrorism; and for all who work for peace, justice and
the restoration of community life where it has been
undermined or destroyed.
May your Spirit inspire all who seek to bring good out of evil and
hope where there is despair.

We pray for those struggling to deal with unwelcome news and life
events:
for those who are ill, and those who have been bereaved;
for those who have lost their work and their confidence.
May they all find your strength and grace through the work of
those who counsel and minister to them.

We pray for those moving home and leaving family, friends and
familiar surroundings:
for those having to move to seek security and safety;
for old people leaving their homes to live in nursing and
community homes.
May they all find you present with them now and in the days to
come.

We pray for the life of the church:
for all who proclaim the gospel in word and deed;
for our relations with people of other Christian traditions;
for those of other faiths, especially those with whom we share
our daily life.
May the gifts of the Spirit live and grow in our communities.

We remember all who have died, asking that they may find
eternal life.
God of grace, since in your love for us, our concerns are also yours,
be present in your power with all for whom we pray.
We ask this through Christ the Lord.   **Amen**

Dismissal

The Lord our God grant you a spirit of thankfulness,
and grace to serve him always.
May his name be ever on your lips, and in your heart.   **Amen**

4th Sunday after Epiphany

Theme

God fills all things with his presence, uniting earth and heaven in unending praise in Christ our Lord.

Call to Worship

The Lord of hosts is with us;
Surely the Lord is in this place.
Let us worship the Lord our God.

Prayer of Adoration

Eternal God, present in all times and places, yet limited by none,
to you belongs the praise of all peoples, the blessing of every generation.
Though the heavens cannot contain you, in Christ you dwell among your people by the power of your Spirit.
May the praises of young and old resound to your glory, with all on earth and in heaven, now, and in eternity,
through Christ our Lord.   **Amen**

Prayer of Thanksgiving

Let us remember God's providential care of all creation and his presence with us and all his people.
We give thanks:
for particular places where we have found God's holy presence;
for all who have cared for the worship and service of God;
for this place of worship and the people of God in this area;
for God's grace and love towards us from past days until now;
for reassurance and guidance in times of uncertainty and doubt.
God of Abraham and Sarah, Isaac and Jacob,
in mercy and faithfulness you have watched over your people.
Be always a present help to us and all who call upon your name;
for yours is the honour, thanksgiving and love,
now and in all ages, through Jesus Christ our Lord.   **Amen**

Prayer of Intercession

This response may be used in this prayer:
L: Lord of earth and heaven: R: **Hear our prayer.**

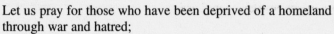

United with all who serve God on earth and in heaven,
let us offer our prayers to him, through Christ our Lord:

Let us pray for those who have been deprived of a homeland
through war and hatred;
    for those who are homeless, and those without work;
    for all those seeking meaning and purpose in their lives.
    May they find safety, accommodation, employment and faith.

Let us pray for all God's people, particularly for the children of
Abraham, that, as they are able, Jews, Muslims, and Christians may
be living signs of God's holy presence in the world.

Let us pray for all who seek God's presence in their wilderness of
trial and suffering:
    for the sick and all who care for them;
    for the mentally and physically disabled;
    and for those who are bereaved.
And let us remember all who have died and who now find a home
in God.

Gracious God, you hear the prayers of all those who turn to you in
faith. May what we ask in the name of Christ, your Son, be
accomplished according to your will,
through the same Christ our Lord.   **Amen**

Dismissal

May God go with you and guide you;
may you find his presence always with you;
may your lives be filled with his grace and peace,
through Jesus Christ our Lord.   **Amen**

5th Sunday after Epiphany

Theme

Through all the ages of human history, God has never been without witnesses to his presence.

Call to Worship

Open our eyes, O God, to your presence,
that we may see and know
what prophets and seers long desired
which you have revealed
in the fullness of time
in Jesus Christ our Lord.

Prayer of Confession

This response may be used in this prayer:
L: Lord have mercy: R: **Christ have mercy.**

In God's presence, let us call to mind how we have failed to serve him and others, and let us ask God's forgiveness.
Lord our God, you have called us, yet we have refused your call.
We have been unappreciative of your gifts, worshipping your creation and forgetting you, the Creator;
We have disregarded your truth and your call to repentance and healing;
We have turned our hearts from you, lacking perception of your grace and of the needs of others;
Gracious God,
you promise pardon and peace to all who turn in faith to you.
Forgive our sins, set us free from our faults, and raise us to new life,
through the offering and prayer of Jesus Christ our Lord.   **Amen**

Prayer of Intercession

By the grace of God's Spirit, let us offer our prayers:
We pray for all for whom the vision of a ruined city is a reality:
    those living in areas devastated by war,
    in shattered houses and destroyed neighbourhoods.
We pray for those whose livelihood has been taken away:
    those whose land has been ruined and laid waste,
    those whose goods have been appropriated by others.
We pray for captives who have been removed far from their homes
    and all who work and pray for their freedom.
We pray for all who seek to proclaim a prophetic word
    in national and international politics,
    through the work of aid and development agencies.
We pray for all who go for us to proclaim good news to the poor,
    to bring healing and wholeness to the sick,
    to support basic human rights where they are denied.
We pray for all who deal in arms, and all who have control of
nuclear weapons;
    for all who work in decommissioning nuclear facilities;
    that they may ever be mindful of the threat such weapons pose to
    the future of all.
We pray for the church of God
    that the peace of Christ may rule in our hearts and minds;
    that all Christians may work for peace and reconciliation, as
    signs of the kingdom of God.
Lord, grant to us and all your people a vision of a new heaven and
a new earth;
Give us grace, that we may set our hearts on a future for all, which
reflects your kingdom of justice, righteousness and truth;
By your Holy Spirit, turn the minds of those for whom we pray
towards those things that belong to their peace and the good of all,
through Jesus Christ our Lord.   **Amen**

Offering Prayer

Lord, give us wisdom, that these gifts we offer and the lives we
offer with them, may be used to build, not to destroy, to bring new
life and hope, by your grace and power through Jesus Christ our
Lord.   **Amen**

6th Sunday after Epiphany

Theme

God feeds and sustains us in his love and mercy.
We may find his goodness in his gifts to us, and his presence with us
in our lives.

Call to Worship

This is the day which the Lord has made
Let us be glad and rejoice in it.

Prayer of Confession

This response may be used in this prayer:
L: Lord forgive us: **R: Help us to forgive**.

God of kindness and compassion, you bear with the sins of your
people, that they may turn to you in repentance and faith. Hear us
as we confess to you:

We have forgotten your goodness and resented the good of another:
We have forgotten that you require mercy and not sacrifice, and
preferred harsh legalism to your grace:
We have been selfish and unmindful of the needs of others,
intolerant of them and lacking in patience:
We have judged others, forgetting that in so doing we ourselves are
judged:

Lord, as we live by your forgiving grace,
keep us mindful of our Saviour's word,
that forgiven much, we too may forgive,
through him who died for our sins and rose again for us,
Christ our Lord.   **Amen**

Prayer of Intercession

This response may be used in this prayer:
L: God of love: R: **Be a present help to them**.

Let us bring to God the needs of the world and the church, and ask
for grace to serve him in our daily life.
Loving God,
Give hope and perseverance to all who are in need,
 be near to those in sickness or in sorrow,
 and restore them to wholeness of life;
Give bread to those who are hungry;
 care, and an sense of obligation for justice
 to those who live in plenty;
Grant wisdom and sensitivity to all who make our laws,
 and to those who frame rules and regulations;
 may their work lead us to a life that is more humane and just for
 all.
Father,
Help us who offer these prayers to offer our lives with them, that
by your grace, that which we pray for we may effectively work for,
that your will may be done, through Jesus Christ our Lord.   **Amen**

Meditation

The bread of the eucharist is Christ's bread.
Reflect today on the barriers which prevent restored eucharistic
communion between all baptized Christians.
Pray that the communion of the church may be healed, that
Christians may in one body, share one bread.

Dismissal

May your days be filled with the presence of the Lord;
may he lead you, with all his people, to the joy and peace of his
kingdom.   **Amen**

9th Sunday before Easter

Theme

God calls us to be people of the beatitudes, signs of his love in Christ to all the world.

Call to Worship

Happy are those who wait upon the Lord, their strength and hope will be renewed.

Prayer of Confession

This response may be used in this prayer:
L: Lord: R: **Have mercy.**

God alone knows us in the depths of our being.
Let us call to mind our sins, in which we have failed to love God and others, and let us ask God to forgive us.
For the hurt we did not mean to cause others, and the hurt we meant to cause;
for the words we did not mean to speak, and the words we meant to say;
for the dislike and hatred we did not mean to show, and the love we did not show.
God of justice, forgive our sins;
as you show mercy to us, so help us to be merciful,
that we may live according to your word,
through Jesus Christ our Lord.   **Amen**

Prayer of Intercession

This response may be used in this prayer:
L: Lord, we look to you: R: **Save and help us.**

Let us pray
that the people of the Old and New Covenants may rejoice in their common heritage of faith;
that God will gather the church throughout the world in greater unity in diversity;
that all Christians may discover the gifts God has given them to

serve him;
that we may witness for the gospel in love, fidelity and purity;
for all who share the bread of affliction and the water of adversity,
that those in sorrow may find consolation;
for all who hunger and thirst to see right prevail;
for all who make peace where there is conflict;
for all who are persecuted for conscience's sake;
for all who are insulted and decried for the testimony they bear to
the truth;
for all who have died, that they may share the eternal life of God's
kingdom.

To you, Lord God, we come for help,
Show us your mercy and your favour,
that we may rejoice to tell of your saving power
through Jesus Christ our Lord.   **Amen**

Offering Prayer

To the poor in spirit is given the kingdom of heaven;
    those of a gentle spirit inherit the earth;
To those who suffer for your name, you promise your kingdom;
    those who follow you above all else will find a treasure beyond
    price.
Lord, we remember these graces beyond our deserving
    as we offer our gifts to you.   **Amen**

Meditation

God calls us in Christ to be people of the Beatitudes.
These hallmarks of God's kingdom reflect our being and attitudes.
How our lives are shaped according to the gospel reveals how
central its values are to us, and our witness enables those around us
to find meaning in the good news.

8th Sunday before Easter

Theme

In Christ we are caught up into the love of God, that in it we may find
wholeness and healing for the world.

Call to Worship

Come, praise the Lord our God,
who by his grace gives life to all
and whose power is made perfect in our weakness.

Prayer of Adoration

Praise to you, the God of all the earth,
for you make your presence known
in the wonder of creation;
through Israel your people;
and in your love and mercy
in Jesus Christ your Son.
By your Spirit
you create among us
a living fire of communion
in which our lives
are caught up into your eternity.
Glory to you, O Lord, now and for ever.   **Amen**

Prayer of Intercession

This response may be used in this prayer.
L: By the grace of your Spirit: R: **Strengthen them.**

Let us ask God's grace for all in need:
God, whose grace is sufficient for all our need, we pray:
for all who are passing through a time of weakness;
for all who seek healing;
for all who live with disability;
for all whom you call to serve you;
for those who need faith and courage
   in facing persecution and hardship;

for those whose needs are known to you alone;

Father of all,
to whom none are strangers,
but all are known;
hear our prayers
and enable us to do your will
in all that you ask of us,
that your purposes of truth and love
may be fulfilled in us
and in all for whom we pray,
through Jesus Christ our Lord.   **Amen**

Offering Prayer

Lord, we offer you
our gifts in thanksgiving,
our hands to work for you,
our lives in your service,
in the name of Christ.   **Amen**

Dismissal

Go and tell what you have heard and seen;
the blind see;
the lame walk;
the sick are made whole;
the poor hear good news;
the dead are raised to eternal life.
These are the signs of God's kingdom.
Go, proclaim the gospel of Christ our Lord.   **Amen**

7th Sunday before Easter

Theme

God is our saviour and deliverer. In times of disaster and suffering
God is ever near to us in Christ, to show us his mercy.

Call to Worship

The Lord is a God of justice:
Happy are those who wait for him.

Prayer of Confession

This response may be used in this prayer:
L: Lord: R: **Hear us and save us**.

Holy and forgiving God,
we come to you, that we may see your goodness and mercy.
We have turned from you, our maker and redeemer;
We have refused to listen to your word
    and your call to obedience;
We have imagined you are hidden from us
    and blind to our words and deeds;
We have preferred our own illusions
    to your truth;
We have rejected the quietness and confidence
    of your strength;
God of love and mercy,
have compassion on us;
free us from our fears and sins
to live as those whom you call your children
through Jesus Christ our Lord.   **Amen**

Prayer of Intercession

This response may be used in this prayer:
L: Save us Lord: R: **Show us your mercy.**

Let us offer our prayers to God.
We remember in God's presence all who are imprisoned for

conscience's sake. We ask God to uphold and support them,
  and all those who work to see justice prevail.
We remember all who persecute the church,
  all who are our enemies,
  and we pray for all Christians living under unjust regimes;
  be present with them in their time of trial.
We remember those who seek freedom for the oppressed
  and hope for the despairing.
We remember the saints and martyrs
  who lived and died in faithfulness to the gospel,
  asking that we may follow their examples of faithful witness.
We remember the Christian communities of our neighbourhood;
  unite us and guide us in love for one another.

God our Saviour,
come to the help of your people
who place their hope and trust in you.
As we recall your saving power
in your mighty acts,
may those for whom we pray
know your presence with them,
and your help in time of need
through Jesus Christ our Lord.   **Amen**

Offering Prayer

Lord God, we recall your love for us in all that you have done,
from the beginning of creation until now.
May these gifts we offer, and the lives offered with them,
declare your love for all the world,
in Jesus Christ our Lord.   **Amen**

Dismissal

May God, who in Jesus Christ
  called the disciples to witness to his mighty deeds,
  give you grace to tell of his saving power.   **Amen**

6th Sunday before Easter
Lent 1

Deut. 30.15–22
James 1.12–18
Matt. 4.1–11

Presentation

The Gospel story lends itself to dramatic presentation, such as a mime, a simple dance, or a reading for three voices.

Call to Worship

Jesus said:
'It is written:
"Worship the Lord your God
and serve only him." '
Let us worship God.

Prayer of Confession

God of love,
we confess to you our many sins.
We often know what we should do
but fail to do it.
We find temptation hard to resist.
Because your Son our Lord Jesus Christ
was tempted just as we are,
we know that you understand our weakness
and that you still love us
and are ready to forgive us.
Forgive us now, we pray,
and help us to fight against temptation;
through Jesus Christ our Lord.   **Amen**

Prayer of Thanksgiving

God our creator, to you be thanks and praise.
You made the universe
and you made each one of us.
L: For all your mighty acts:
R: **We give you thanks and praise.**

God our Father, to you be thanks and praise.
You sent your Son Jesus Christ
to be the Saviour of the world.
We thank you for his life
and for the example that he gave us.
We thank you that he overcame temptation
and helps us to choose what is right.
We thank you that he died on the cross
and that you raised him to life again.
We thank you for the Holy Spirit,
who guides and strengthens us.
L: For all your mighty acts:
R: **We give you thanks and praise**.
Through Jesus Christ our Lord.   **Amen**

Prayer of Intercession

Strong and wise God,   \
we pray for all who face temptation:
for those in positions of authority
who are tempted to misuse their power;
for those, ill and depressed,
who are tempted to lose hope;
for those in your church
who are tempted to abandon Christ's way.
And we pray for ourselves
that, when we are tempted to do wrong,
we may turn from evil and do good,
strengthened by your Spirit;
through Jesus Christ our Lord.   **Amen**

Dismissal and Blessing

Go in peace. Love the Lord your God, conform to his ways, and
keep his commandments.
And the blessing …

5th Sunday before Easter
Lent 2

Isa. 35.1–10
I John 3.1–10
Matt. 12.22–32

Presentation

*All members of the congregation, whatever their ages, will have
some experience and awareness of evil in today's world. Try to show
how the Bible readings have contemporary significance for us.*

Call to Worship

God is our refuge and strength,
an ever-present help in trouble.
Let us worship God.

Prayer of Adoration

God of truth and grace,
we worship and adore you.
All wisdom and power are yours;
all goodness comes from you.
You made the world in your love;
you care for all your children.
God of truth and grace,
we worship and adore you;
through Jesus Christ our Lord.   **Amen**

Prayer of Confession

God our Father,
we are sorry for all that is wrong in our lives.
We think too much of ourselves
and too little about you.
We put ourselves before other people.
We give in too easily to temptation
and compromise with evil.
But you are full of compassion and love.
You are ready and willing to forgive us.
Help us to know that you love and accept us
and that you have forgiven our sins;
through Jesus Christ our Lord.   **Amen**

Prayer of Thanksgiving

God of all-redeeming grace,
we give you thanks and praise.
You care for all your creation
and you love each one of us.
L: With joyful hearts: R: **We thank you, God of grace.**

When we had fallen into sin,
you sent your Son to be our Saviour.
He lived on earth,
full of grace and truth.
He fought against evil
and taught us what is good.
L: With joyful hearts: R: **We thank you, God of grace**.

He died on the cross
and was raised again,
victorious over sin and death.
You have sent your Spirit
to be with the church for ever
and to help us in our fight against evil.
L: With joyful hearts: R: **We thank you, God of grace**.

Through Jesus Christ our Lord.   **Amen**

Dismissal

Be strong, be resolute,
for the Lord your God is with you.
Go in peace.

4th Sunday before Easter
Lent 3

Presentation

*The emphasis today is not on suffering in general, but on the
sufferings of Christ and those who suffer for his sake. This is a
difficult theme for all-age worship, but we must not keep it from the
young. It must, however, be handled sensitively and not luridly.*

Call to Worship

Jesus began to make it clear to his disciples that he had to go to
Jerusalem and endure great suffering.
By his wounds we are healed.
Let us worship God.

Prayer of Confession

God of our salvation,
as we remember the sufferings
of our Lord Jesus Christ,
we confess our sins to you.
We have been selfish and greedy;
we have hurt you and one another;
we have not wanted to take up our cross
and follow Jesus.
We are sorry that we have been poor disciples.
Trusting in your love,
we ask you to forgive us
and help us to be better followers of Jesus;
for his sake.   **Amen**

Prayer of Intercession

God of love,
we pray for the church throughout the world,
and especially for Christians
who suffer persecution and hardship
simply because they follow Jesus.
L: God of love: R: **Hear our prayer.**

We pray for the nations of the world,
and especially for those who suffer
as a result of prejudice, conflict and war.
L: God of love: R: **Hear our prayer.**

We pray for those in need,
and especially for those who suffer
illness of body or mind.
L: God of love: R: **Hear our prayer.**

We thank you for all your saints,
and especially those who have died as martyrs,
witnesses to Christ.
We pray that we,
inspired by their example
and strengthened by their fellowship,
may come to be with them
in your eternal kingdom.
L: God of love: R: **Hear our prayer.**

We ask our prayers through Jesus Christ our Lord.   **Amen**

Offering Prayer

Lord our God,
your Son Jesus Christ gave up his life for us.
We offer these gifts
as signs of our love and gratitude
and our dedication of our lives to you;
through Jesus our Saviour.   **Amen**

Dismissal

L: Let us go out to love and serve the Lord.
R: **Let us take up our cross and follow Jesus.**   **Amen**

3rd Sunday before Easter
Lent 4

Presentation

The story of the Transfiguration may appropriately be treated in all-age worship as an experience of revelation which enabled the three disciples to see Jesus in a new way. One could lead up to this by showing a picture which can be interpreted in more than one way. Things are not always what they seem!

Call to Worship

May God be gracious to us and bless us.
May he cause his face to shine upon us.
Let us worship God.

Prayer of Adoration

Eternal, majestic God,
creator of life and light,
you bring order out of chaos
and light out of darkness.
We praise and adore you.
All glory and majesty,
wisdom and authority
belong to you, now and for ever.   **Amen**

Prayer of Confession

God our Father,
we confess our sins to you.
We have glimpsed your glory
but have chosen darkness rather than light.
L: Father: R: **Forgive us.**
We have heard your voice calling us
but we have not listened.
L: Father: R: **Forgive us.**
We have claimed to follow Jesus
but we have gone our own way.
L: Father: R: **Forgive us.**

Help us to know that we are loved and forgiven
and to walk in the light of your love;
through Jesus Christ our Lord.   **Amen**

Prayer of Thanksgiving

God of grace and glory,
we give you thanks and praise.
We thank you for the world around us,
showing your creative power.
We thank you for the life of Jesus,
making known your merciful goodness.
We thank you for his death and resurrection,
revealing your mighty victory
over sin and death.
We thank you for the Holy Spirit,
enlightening our minds with your truth.
God of grace and glory,
we give you thanks and praise;
through Jesus Christ our Lord.   **Amen**

Dismissal and Blessing

As we leave this place of worship
to serve God in the world,
the glory of the Lord goes with us.
The Lord bless you and keep you.
The Lord make his face to shine on you
and be gracious to you.
The Lord look on you with kindness
and give you peace.   **Amen**

Mothering Sunday

Presentation

Images (e.g. Matt. 23.37) and stories can draw out different aspects of mothering: protection, warmth, feeding, nursing, teaching, discipline. Link Romans with news of our own 'benefactors and co-workers' especially women and the prayers of intercession.

Call to Worship

'As a mother comforts her child
so shall I myself comfort you', says the Lord.
Let us worship God.

Prayer of Confession

The Lord is compassionate and merciful;
slow to anger, and abounding in steadfast love.
Let us confess to God
   our failures in love and service;
   and let us ask forgiveness for our sins.   *Silence*
May God who comforts us
as a mother comforts her children,
forgive and reconcile us,
and enfold us in mercy,
in Jesus Christ our Lord.   **Amen**

Prayer of Thanksgiving

O loving God, we thank you
that your care for us is tender and gentle and strong,
surrounding us like a hug, cradling us like supporting arms.
We thank you that you understand our problems,
even the private, difficult things
that we cannot explain to other people;
and that, because you understand,
we do not have to be worried, and we do not have to be afraid.

We thank you that your wisdom guides us from day to day,
calling us to care for others as you care for us,
to forgive others as you forgive us,
so that every one may know themselves
to be held in your embracing love,
this day and always.   **Amen**

Prayer of Intercession

L: For all mothers and for every human family:
R: **We pray in faith.**
L: For the church in every country and for all God's children:
R: **We pray in faith.**
L: For the world God loves and for justice and peace among the
nations:
R: **We pray in faith.**
L: For the sick and the sorrowful and for all in trouble and need:
R: **We pray in faith.**
L: We pray in the name of Jesus Christ our Lord.   **Amen**

Dismissal

God, who cares for you like a mother, will be with you during the
coming days,
    to enable and encourage,
    to shelter and protect,
    to nourish and inspire.
Go with confidence, with joy and with hope.   **Amen**

Gen. 25.29–34
Rom. 8.1–11
Matt. 20.20–28

2nd Sunday before Easter
Lent 5   Passion Sunday

Presentation

The Christian Year supplies a perceptible change of mood today, for this is 'the First Sunday of the Passion' (Passion Sunday). We begin to focus much more clearly on the sufferings of Christ as our preparation for Holy Week, especially Good Friday, intensifies. To achieve the solemnity appropriate to the season without making worship dull and boring is not easy, especially in all age worship, but the attempt should be made.

Call to Worship

The Son of Man did not come to be served, but to serve,
and to give up his life as a ransom for many.
Let us worship God.

Prayer of Confession

Merciful God,
we confess our failings and failures.
We have been half-hearted disciples of Jesus.
We have sung his praises
but we have not followed in his steps.
We have not been willing to take up the cross.
We have not served others as he has served us.
We ask you to forgive us
and to help us to be better disciples;
for the sake of Jesus Christ our Lord.   **Amen**

Prayer of Thanksgiving

Eternal God, we thank you for your goodness and mercy
which follow us all the days of our life.
We thank you for the world you created
and for making us, male and female, in your own image.
We thank you for your patience with us
and your kindness towards us:

though we rebelled against you
you sent your Son to draw us back to you.
Taking the form of a servant, he humbled himself,
accepting even death on a cross.
In his living and his dying,
he showed us the greatness of service,
the strength of weakness and the power of love.
You have raised him from death and exalted him in heaven.
In his name you have sent your Holy Spirit
to strengthen us for service.
For all your acts of grace and love we praise and thank you
now and for ever;
through Jesus Christ our Lord.   **Amen**

Offering Prayer

You give us so much, Father:
life itself, our time, talents and resources;
our families and friends;
and you have given your Son to serve and save the world.
In gratitude for your many gifts,
we offer our lives to you
that we may serve you and others
to the glory of your name;
through Jesus Christ our Saviour.   **Amen**

Dismissal

Go out in the name of Jesus.
Take up your cross and follow him.
Be servants of others
as Christ was the servant of all.
And know that he is with you, now and always.   **Amen**

Sunday before Easter
Lent 6   Palm Sunday

Presentation

It should be possible to have a procession today. If this cannot be done outdoors, why not have a procession inside the building, perhaps while 'All glory, laud and honour' is being sung? Palm crosses are a superb visual aid, reminding us that Palm Sunday is not only a celebration of Christ's triumphal entry into Jerusalem but also the first day of Holy Week, with the Cross only days ahead. The last verse of 'Ride on, ride on in majesty' admirably expresses this dual emphasis.

Call to Worship

Hosanna to the Son of David!
Blessed is he who comes in the name of the Lord.
Hosanna in the highest!

Palm Prayer

When the palm crosses have been distributed, all hold them in the air, as the leader says this prayer:

God of glory,
whose Son Jesus Christ entered Jerusalem
to suffer and to die:
may these palms be for us
signs of his victory;
and may we honour you
by acclaiming him as our king
and following him in the way that leads to eternal life;
for his sake.   **Amen**

Prayer of Confession

We ask your forgiveness, merciful God,
for we share in the sin of the world.
Though we claim to follow Jesus,
we go our own way.

Though we joyfully sing 'Hosanna',
our lives shout 'Crucify him'.
Though we promise to be faithful,
our words and deeds betray him.
We are truly sorry for our sins.
As we turn to you now, in penitence and faith,
help us to know that you love and forgive us
and enable us to make a new start;
for the sake of Jesus Christ our Lord.   **Amen**

Prayer of Intercession

L: For the city of Jerusalem
  and for all who live there:
R: **We pray to the Lord.**
L: For our own city (town, village)
  and for this local community:
R: **We pray to the Lord.**
L: For the sick and the sorrowful and for all who care for them:
R: **We pray to the Lord.**
L: For the church throughout the world and for all Christian people:
R: **We pray to the Lord;**
L: Through Jesus Christ our Lord.   **Amen**

Dismissal

Let us go in peace
to follow Jesus
on the way that leads to the cross
and onward to eternal life.
Hosanna in the highest!   **Amen**

Easter Day

Presentation

Easter Day is the most important and joyful day in the church's calendar. The mood is one of celebration: Christ is risen! Lots of flowers, an Easter candle and other visible ways of contrasting the joy of Easter with the austerity of Lent will help to create an appropriate atmosphere. The Easter Gospel may effectively be read by three or four voices (one or two narrators, Jesus and Mary.) It is best to omit prayers of confession on Easter Day.

Call to Worship

L: Alleluia! Christ is risen!
R: **He is risen indeed! Alleluia!**

Prayer of Adoration

We praise you,
God and Father of our Lord Jesus Christ.
By your great mercy
we have been born anew to a living hope
for you have raised your Son from the dead.
In his name, we praise and adore you.
Alleluia!   **Amen**

Prayer of Thanksgiving

God of power and love,
we join with saints and angels
to celebrate your mighty acts.
We thank you for your creation
and for the signs of spring in the world about us,
reminding us of your renewing work.
We thank you for your mightiest act,
in raising Jesus from the dead.
We thank you that he has overcome sin and death for us
and brought us life and hope.

We thank you for all your faithful people
whose lives have revealed your transforming power.
We praise your holy name
and rejoice in your wonderful deeds;
through Jesus Christ our Lord.   **Amen**

Prayer of Petition

L: Jesus called Mary by name and she knew that he was risen.
Silence
   Help us to hear your voice:
R: **Come to us, risen Lord Jesus.**

L: Jesus came to his disciples and said 'Peace be with you.'
Silence
   Help us to know your peace:
R: **Come to us, risen Lord Jesus.**

L: Jesus appeared to Thomas and overcame his doubts.
Silence
   Help us to believe:
R: **Come to us, risen Lord Jesus**.

L: Jesus broke bread with two disciples in Emmaus and they
   recognized their Lord.
Silence
   Help us to know your presence with us always:
R: **Come to us, risen Lord Jesus.   Amen**

Dismissal

Go out into the world with joy,
and know that the risen Christ is with you.
Alleluia!   **Amen**

1st Sunday after Easter

Presentation

Too many Christians seem to think that Easter is over in a day. In fact the great Fifty Days of Easter extend to Pentecost and the joyful character of the season continues throughout. Today's Gospel could be dramatized: a short sketch based upon it, emphasizing the desperate but futile measures of those who wanted to 'disprove' the resurrection, could be very helpful.

Call to Worship

L: Alleluia! Christ is risen!
R: **He is risen indeed! Alleluia!**

Prayer of Adoration

Glory be to you, Lord God;
you raised your Son from the dead.
Glory be to you, Lord Jesus Christ;
you live and reign for ever.
Glory be to you, Holy Spirit;
you breathe new life into God's people.
Glory be to you, Father, Son and Holy Spirit.
Alleluia!   **Amen**.

Prayer of Intercession

Let us pray for the church of Christ
that all Christian people
may be faithful witnesses to the resurrection.
Silence
L: Lord of all: R: **Hear our prayer**.
Let us pray for the peoples of the world
and the leaders of the nations
that peace may replace war, love may conquer hatred,
and hope may banish despair.
Silence
L: Lord of all: R: **Hear our prayer**.

Let us pray for those who mourn
and for those who are sick
that they may be comforted and strengthened
by faith in the living Christ.
Silence
L: Lord of all: R: **Hear our prayer**.
Let us thank God for the saints in light,
whose lives and deaths bore witness
to the power and love of Christ;
and let us pray that we may come to share with them
in the joy of God's eternal kingdom.
Silence
L: Lord of all: R: **Hear our prayer**.
We ask this for the sake of Jesus Christ our Lord.   **Amen**

Offering Prayer

You are worthy, glorious God,
to receive blessing and honour and praise.
We can never give you enough
to show how much we love you.
But we offer these gifts as signs of our love
and we pray that our lives,
offered in your service,
may be used for your glory;
through Jesus Christ our Lord.   **Amen**

Dismissal

In the name of Christ, crucified and risen,
go into the world with joy,
and be witnesses that Christ is risen.
Alleluia!   **Amen**

I Kings 17.17–24
Col. 3.1–11
Matt. 12.38–42

2nd Sunday after Easter

Presentation

*Focus on the 'Easter Surprise' with illustrations of things renewed,
restored (see I Kings 17.22), hidden (Col. 3.3), concealed, found in
unexpected places. Because of Easter, life has meaning and potential
beyond our imagining. How do we live it?*

Call to Worship   (*Col. 3.1*)

If then you have been raised with Christ
seek the things that are above,
where Christ is, seated at the right hand of God.

Prayer of Adoration

O God of glory, we adore you for your greatness. Because there is
power to raise the dead, to restore what is fractured, divided, lost,
all good is possible. We adore you for your grace. Because death is
not the end of life, we are born anew to a potential beyond our
dreams. We adore you.

Prayer of Confession

O God of life, we are sorry that we are so slow to let go of those
thoughts and words and deeds which we know are wrong. Because
you love us, we know they are unworthy; because you strengthen
us, we know they have no power over us. And yet we hold on to
them. Forgive us, Lord, our reluctance to walk the new way, to live
the new life. Help us to choose the right, so that day by day we
may grow in what is good and true and just.   **Amen**

Prayer of Thanksgiving

O God of tomorrow, we give you thanks that your love is
recreating us to live as your children. We praise you that your love
has dealt with all that is wrong in us and in the world, and that we
are called to make real your promises through kind words and
brave deeds.

We bless you that your love is present with us, lifting us up, helping us on, urging us towards the light of your truth and the wonder of your kingdom, this day and forever.   **Amen**

Prayer of Intercession

Loving Father, may your new life flow like a river through us, our church, our community, the whole world.

L: Lord, we are your children: R: **Live in us today.**
We pray for each other, especially those who are sad, lonely, troubled or in pain. May we bear each others' burdens.

L: Lord, we are your children: R: **Live in us today.**
We pray for our church, especially for those who teach and minister among us. May we become more open to your renewing power.

L: Lord, we are your children: R: **Live in us today.**
We pray for our neighbourhood, especially for those people who cannot grow in love. May we care for them.

L: Lord, we are your children: R: **Live in us today.**
We pray for our world, especially for those countries where there is hunger or war. May we stand for justice and be bearers of your peace.

L: Lord, we are your children: R: **Live in us today.**

Offering Prayer

Lord, with grateful hearts we offer ourselves (with these our gifts ...) to the service of your kingdom. Humble our souls to hear your voice, so that, inspired to seek the greater glory, we may live in wonder, praise and joy.   **Amen**

Dismissal

Go in peace. Walk the new way. Live the new life.
And be prepared for God's surprises!

3rd Sunday after Easter

Presentation

Visual aids can focus on the living body (many parts, unity, all working together for the common good) or on the activity of building (foundations, the humility of materials, skills, the common purpose). Both are signs of life.

Call to Worship   (*John 11.25–26a*)

Jesus said to her 'I am the resurrection and the life; he who believes in me, though he die, yet shall he live, and whoever lives and believes in me shall never die.'

Prayer of Adoration

O God of Life, yours is the power which forged the universe, giving life to creatures large and small, delighting to create wonders, and marking out our planet as a garden for your joy. We adore you.

O God of Life, yours is the love involved in creation, committed to our well-being. All that you have, all that you are, you have given – still give – to claim back the heights and the depths of our humanity, and to form us as a people of praise. We adore you.

O God of Life, yours is the energy making all things new, strengthening the weak and healing the broken, to build on earth, to build amongst us, a temple to your name, and a kingdom for your glory. We adore you.

Prayer of Confession and Thanksgiving

Loving God, we are sorry we have resisted your grace, and obstructed your purposes. Not recognizing your Spirit at work in each other, we have built walls of intolerance instead of gates of vision or doors of exploration.

Forgive us, Lord, that we expect so little when there is so much that you want to give. Forgive us that we are content with death, when you want to give us life.

O God of Life, yours is the power which raised Jesus from the dead, which breaks into our everyday, gathering the fragments of our lives into hope beyond our imagining, a future beyond our dreams. We praise your holy name.

Prayer of Intercession

O God, you are present in our midst. We pray for each other, especially those who are troubled or in need at this time (for ...). Help us to work together for the common good.
L: Build us in your love: R: **Lead us into life**.

O God, you call us to minister to those who are anxious, lonely or sick. We pray for our neighbours and friends (for ...). Help us to love others so that they may become whole.
L: Build us in your love: R: **Lead us into life**.

O God, you call us to receive your gifts for service in the Body of Christ. We pray for those who minister among us (for ...). May we be open to the Spirit and willing to share what we receive.
L: Build us in your love: R: **Lead us into life**.

O God, you call us to build each other up in love and wisdom. We pray for those who have been brought low or broken (for ...). Raise them up, loving Father, and gather us all into your new day.
Amen

Offering Prayer

Living God, may all that we offer be used for the common good: to encourage your people, give love to our neighbours, build up your kingdom, bring hope to the world, this day and forever.   **Amen**

Dismissal

L: Lead us into life!   R: **Lead us into life!**
L: Lead us into love!   R: **Lead us into love!**
L: Lead us as your Body!   R: **Lead us as your Body!**
L: Build us as your Temple!   R: **Build us as your Temple!**
L: Lead us into praise!   R: **Lead us into praise!**

4th Sunday after Easter

Presentation

*Tell the story of David and Jonathan (I Sam. 18–20; II Sam. 1).
Discuss the nature of friendship. List the qualities of the true friend.
Relate these to the way God loves us.*

Call to Worship   *(I John 2.8)*

'Yet I am writing you a new commandment, which is true in him
and in you, because the darkness is passing away and the true light
is already shining.'

Prayer of Thanksgiving

O God of the Pilgrim Way, we thank you that through many
generations you have kept faith with your people. You have
remained bound by your covenant, you have always worked for our
deliverance. Yours is a steadfast love which is always there, ready
to provide for our deepest needs. We give you thanks and praise.

   O Living Christ, we thank you that whatever we do, wherever
we go, you walk with us as our light and our example, sharing our
sorrows and our joys; knowing the truth of us; understanding the
things that bear down on us making it difficult to choose the right.
Yours is a steadfast love which has never left us to suffer alone, but
is always making space for us to be ourselves. We give you thanks
and praise.

   O Companion Spirit, we thank you that you still keep faith with
us, that yours are arms from which we cannot fall, yours is a love
which will not let us go, but which travels with us, serving us,
trusting us, and teaching us to serve and trust others in return.
Yours is a steadfast love, which has never failed us, but is always
waiting, willing to make us feel at home. We give you thanks and
praise.

Prayer of Intercession

O God of Love, you are friend to the whole world;
standing with us in our pain, pleading for justice, mercy and peace,
humbly offering yourself to deal with our sin.
    We pray for the world (especially for …).
O God of Love, you are friend to the church;
helping us to grow in compassion and knowledge, devotion and
obedience,
humbly offering yourself to service and to sacrifice.
    We pray for the people of God (especially for …).
O God of Love, you are friend to us;
causing our devotion to be made real in caring,
humbly offering yourself as our companion on the way.
    We pray for each other (especially for …).
O God of Love, you are friend to each one of us,
calling us by name and holding us in your sight,
humbly offering yourself as our way, our truth and our life.
    We pray for ourselves …
O God of Love, holding us in friendship
from the day of our birth to our journey's end,
look kindly upon us as we remember those who have gone ahead
to the home that you have prepared for them.
    In silence we remember them …
And we give you thanks that the love which held them,
surrounds them still, and unites us with them
in one communion of praise, forever offered to your glory.   **Amen**

Offering Prayer

May the father's heart and the Father's authority,
and the Father's work and the Father's life
be made perfect in us through his grace,
this day and forever.

Dismissal

Let us go on our way, finding Christ to be the path we tread.
Let us open our eyes, finding Christ to be the truth which feeds us.
Let us give ourselves, finding Christ to be the life which flows
through us, this day, every day.

5th Sunday after Easter

Presentation

Use stories (e.g. Elijah), 'trust exercises', and personal experience to draw out the meaning of faith as loyalty or 'keeping faith' even in adverse circumstances. Highlight the elements of risk and dependence involved.

Call to Worship   (*Heb. 11.1*)

'Now faith is the assurance of things hoped for, the conviction of things not seen.'

Prayer of Adoration

Heavenly Father, we praise you. Your love for us is constant and sure: strong, to endure for ever; great, to absorb the follies and errors of our ways; patient, to care for us in the tiny details of everyday life.

Glorious Jesus, we praise you. Your life in us is constant and sure: powerful, to deal with evil; caring, to hold us in your prayer; healing, to draw us nearer to God.

Joyous Spirit, we praise you. Your grace in us is constant and sure: steadfast, assuring us God will not change; challenging, calling us to a better hope; sustaining, the seal of an everlasting covenant.

Loving God – Father, Son and Spirit – we give you thanks and praise.

Prayer of Confession

Merciful God, in your love and power you save those who draw near to you through your Son, Jesus Christ our Lord. We are sorry for our faithlessness, our imperfect allegiance, our faltering discipline in service and prayer. Cleanse us and re-make us, so that, purified and renewed in our commitment, we may dedicate ourselves again to your praise.   **Amen**

Prayer of Thanksgiving

O God of faithfulness, as we follow Jesus on the way of
discipleship, we thank you ...
– for the challenge of the choices we must make each day
– for your presence at the perils and pitfalls of the way
– for the humility of our hidden life in you
– for your comfort given in secret,
  your Word nourished in the inner room of our hearts
– for disciplined prayer and devoted service
– for generosity of speech and deed, idea and encouragement.
May we so live with you, that all may see your life enshrined
within us, your love enthroned.

Prayer of Dedication and Intercession

Loving Father, you have seen our need, given from your
abundance, and blessed the work of our hands.
Held within your grace, we pray:
– for all those who seek your kingdom and especially for those
  whose commitment to the cause of right brings them into
  danger ...
– for all who look to you to provide their daily bread,
– for those who give of themselves to serve others ...
– for each other as together we face forgiveness, temptation and
  trial, and venture deeper into loving you, and loving our
  neighbours.
  So receive, here, now, (these tokens of) our lives and our love,
our adoration and our praise, that all may be gathered into your
eternal joy. **Amen**
(*The Lord's Prayer*) Our Father ...

Dismissal

As God has provided, so God will be faithful. As God has
delivered, so God is unchanged. As God holds the days past, so
God holds tomorrow, and all things are blessed by his grace.

6th Sunday after Easter
Sunday after Ascension

Presentation

Illustrate 'idols' with symbols, e.g. money; material wealth (CD player?); status (clerical collar?); power (fat cigar?); education (certificate?); class (school tie?); career (personal organizer?); ideology (Bible?). Contrast with symbols of true worship and service.

Call to Worship   (*John 4.23*)

'But the hour is coming, and now is, when the true worshippers will worship the Father in spirit and truth, for such the Father seeks to worship him.'

Prayer of Thanksgiving

Creator God, we give you thanks and praise that in awesome power you made us, and in tender love you care for us, so that we do not need to be dismayed by change or chance or evil.
L: For you are the true and living God:
R: **You are our everlasting King**.
Saviour Jesus, we give you thanks and praise that in steadfast grace you came into our world, and with fervent love you died and rose in our midst, so that we can trust in your authority to save us from all that is wrong in ourselves, and in others.
L: For you are the true and living God:
R: **You are our everlasting King.**
Holy Spirit, we give you thanks and praise that in constant kindness you bear us up, and with radiant goodness you shine through us, so that we can worship God in Spirit and in truth and spread the Good News of peace and joy.
L: For you are the true and living God:
R: **You are our everlasting King**.
Gracious God, Creator, Saviour, Spirit, we give you thanks and praise that from your truth we receive wisdom in loving, and from your justice, the ability to tell right from wrong. Help us to continue in your way and to grow in your compassion.
L: For you are the true and living God:
R: **You are our everlasting King**.

Prayer of Intercession

O Living God, hear our prayers for your people throughout the world.

– We pray for those you have called to be apostles, to establish and build up new congregations. Strengthen them in faith and in humility.

– We pray for those you have called to be prophets, to challenge us all with your Word and call us to deeper holiness. Strengthen them in courage and in purity of life.

– We pray for those you have called to be evangelists, spreading the Good News of Jesus in word and deed. Strengthen them in listening, understanding and discernment.

– We pray for those you have called to be pastors, offering their hands and their hearts to those in need. Strengthen them in compassion and the power to heal.

– We pray for those you have called to be teachers, studying and explaining the Word to people of all ages. Strengthen them in patience and wisdom.

– We pray for all those you have called to lead your people, to bring others to maturity in spiritual things and equip them for the work of ministry. Strengthen them in stability and vision.

– We pray for ourselves for you have called us all to grow in your Spirit, seeking forbearance and lowliness of heart. Strengthen us in your grace and unite us in peace, that your love may be known and your glory praised, this day and forever.   **Amen**

Offering Prayer

O Christ, you have gone before us to open up the way to the Father. You call us to accept your ministry as our own. Into your hands we place our offerings – praise and thanksgiving, suffering and sacrifice.

May we know them held in your praying love, and see them brought to fulfilment through your powerful grace, now and always.   **Amen**

Dismissal

Go in the grace of Christ who goes ahead of you; in the mercy of the Father who waits to receive you; and in the company of the Spirit who enfolds and empowers you. And may the promise and peace of God be yours forever.   **Amen**

Pentecost

Presentation

List the different images of the Spirit's presence suggested by these readings. What effect do they have? Use visual aids (e.g. windmill, fans) to illustrate the effect of what we cannot see.

Call to Worship

Psalm 42.1–3 or 63.1–4

Prayer of Thanksgiving

O God of glory, we are glad to worship you, for you have poured out your love upon us, like rain on thirsty ground. We give you thanks and praise.

O God of compassion, we are glad to worship you, for you have poured out your mercy upon us, like bread for our hunger. We give you thanks and praise.

O God of friendship, we are glad to worship you, for you have poured out your peace upon us, like days of hope after years of sorrow. We give you thanks and praise.

O God of life, you bring to an end the time of devastation and drought, changing our mourning into dancing, our famine into feasting, our silence into songs of everlasting joy. We give you thanks and praise.

Prayer of Intercession

Sovereign of all Creation, we offer again into your peace those parts of our world which know only hunger, hatred, war. Restore to them the hope that violence has destroyed, and sustain all those who work for justice and reconciliation.

Loving Jesus, our Saviour, we offer again into your compassion those parts of our nation which know only poverty and loneliness. Restore to them the hope that apathy has destroyed, and sustain all those who work to provide home and friendship for all.

Companion Spirit, we offer again into your mercy those parts of ourselves which know only anxiety and fear. Restore to us the joy of your liberating life, and sustain us as we work to bring words and acts of freedom to others.

God of Glory, we offer again into your grace our families and friends, our congregation and our community. Restore to us all the forgiveness which heals the broken, and the faithfulness which perseveres in service and prayer, so that together we may enjoy the wonder of your presence and speak your words of understanding, joy and praise.

Offering Prayer

Living Spirit, we open our hands to receive you.
Help us to wait with patience for your gentle grace.
L: Holy Spirit of God: R: **Move amongst us now.**

Living Spirit, we open our minds to receive you.
Help us to pray with gratitude, penitence and praise.
L: Holy Spirit of God: R: **Move amongst us now.**

Living Spirit, we open our hearts to receive you.
Help us to hear your call to love and to serve.
L: Holy Spirit of God: R: **Move amongst us now.**

Living Spirit, we open our lives to receive you.
Help us to accept the boundless generosity of your care.
L: Holy Spirit of God: R: **Move amongst us now.**

Dismissal

Congregation: **The Living God is with us**:   Leader: Go in peace.
Congregation: **The Living God is with us**:   Leader: Go in love.
Congregation: **The Living God is with us**:   Leader: Go in praise.
Congregation: **The Living God is with us**:   Leader: Go in joy!

1st Sunday after Pentecost
Trinity Sunday

Presentation

Suggest the mystery of God-beyond-us through images of outer space or looking through a microscope. Use the sun as an image of 'sustaining glory' – vast and hot beyond our imagining, yet giving light and warmth.

Call to Worship

Psalm 96.1–3 or Psalm 104.1–4 or Psalm 106.1–2

Prayer of Adoration and Confession

O Living God, Sovereign of the universe, in love you have made us, in love you sustain us day by day. We adore you.

You are the Father who protects us and provides for us; the Son, who lived and died and rose again in our midst; the Spirit, who moves amongst us with energy, like the wind. You are all these, and you are still beyond our hope, our dream. We adore you.

O Living God, as we think of your greatness, we feel very small, and weak, and fragile. As we think of your loving concern for all people, we want to tell you how hard life has been for us. As we think of your forgiveness and mercy, we know we have not always been as loving as we might be.

But you welcome us and you accept us, with a kindness like arms opened wide. Help us to feel the warmth of your understanding love, and to know ourselves held in your friendship for ever.   **Amen**

Prayer of Thanksgiving

Loving Father, you have chosen us to be your children, and given us an inheritance of glory. To us you have revealed your mystery. We give you thanks and praise.
Loving Jesus, you have given yourself to claim us back from evil, so that we can live in grace. To us you have revealed your compassion. We give you thanks and praise.

Loving Spirit, you are poured out upon us as a wonderful blessing, for our help and encouragement. To us you have revealed your wisdom. We give you thanks and praise.
Loving God – Father, Son and Holy Spirit – though you are beyond our understanding, you love us. Though we can barely describe your mercy, you care for us. To us you have revealed yourself in both unity and community. We give you thanks and praise.

Prayer of Dedication and Intercession

God of glory, into your fatherly grace we offer our vision of a world without war, poverty or hunger. We pray for … Grant us faith to share our resources and ourselves. Lead us into a greater trust. Create in us a deeper desire for a true community of nations across the earth.

   L: Lord, in your mercy: R: **Hear our prayer.**

God of glory, into your saving compassion we offer our hope of a nation without homelessness, loneliness or fear. We pray for … Show us how to build new relationships. Help us to serve. Create in us a greater commitment to the common good.

   L: Lord, in your mercy: R: **Hear our prayer**.

God of glory, into your friendly care we offer our picture of a church as the Body of Christ, where we carry each others' joys and sorrows. We pray for … Strengthen us to bear each others' burdens. Teach us to pray. Create in us a longing for true communion with each other and with you.

   L: Lord, in your mercy: R: **Hear our prayer**.

God of glory, into your loving mercy we offer ourselves. May we be always ready to serve you, ever willing to go where you would send us, to bear your message of hope, to carry your good news. **Amen**

Dismissal

May the glory of God – Creator, Saviour and Friend – keep you, guide you and sustain you to live in love and grace, this day and forever. **Amen**

2nd Sunday after Pentecost

Presentation

With swivel chair and powerful lamp illustrate how we 'turn towards the light' to see, read, work etc. Discuss the way that plants will grow and move to find the light. Link with the 'turning' implied in repentance.

Call to Worship   (*Psalm 36.9*)

'For with thee is the fountain of life; in thy light do we see light.'

Prayer of Adoration

O Living God, in the life and ministry of your Son, Jesus Christ,
you are revealed to us as mercy and grace, yet you are still beyond us, your compassion too great for us to fully understand.
All we can do is adore you.
O Living God, in the death and resurrection of your Son, Jesus Christ,
you are revealed to us as forgiveness and love,
yet you are still greater than we can imagine,
your thoughts and ways more wonderful than we can grasp.
All we can do is adore you.

Prayer of Confession

We are sorry, Father God, that when things have gone wrong for us, we have accused you rather than examine ourselves. We have turned out of your narrow way of right living, into the road which leads to wrong, corruption and evil. Turn us around to face the light of your love. Give us a new heart to love you, a new spirit to follow you, so that all our days we may walk in the way of peace. **Amen**

Prayer of Thanksgiving

Leader: For the light that leads us on:
Congregation: **We give you thanks and praise.**
Leader: For the strength which gives us courage:
Congregation: **We give you thanks and praise.**
Leader: For the peace which grows in our hearts:
Congregation: **We give you thanks and praise.**
Leader: For the joy which waits to receive us:
Congregation: **We give you thanks and praise.**

Prayer of Intercession

God of all times and ages, we celebrate the presence of your
kingdom amongst us, in the lives of all those who are leading us
from death into life, from the void into the certain way.

We pray for those who bring us your word of truth, even when
we do not wish to hear it; those who challenge us to radical action
for the sake of right; those who devote themselves to prayer and the
support of others.

God of today and tomorrow, we celebrate the wonder of your
kingdom yet to come in our midst, looking forward with hope to
the fulfilment of your love and joy.

We pray for your church, and for this congregation. May your
truth change us, your grace transform us, and your power renew us,
this day and always.   **Amen**

Offering Prayer

Father, we offer ourselves into your keeping, turning ourselves
towards the light of your love, that your glory may shine on us,
in us, and through us, to the praise of your name, this day and
forever.   **Amen**

Dismissal

Go into the light, walking with the life of God within you.
Go into joy, living with the peace of God in your hearts.
And may the blessing of God …

3rd Sunday after Pentecost

Presentation

Use the congregation's memories of camping, or of war-time blackout, to demonstrate the importance of light for illumination, comfort, warmth, warning, protection, guidance.

Call to worship   *(John 8.12 or 1.1–5)*

Jesus spoke to them, saying, 'I am the light of the world; he who follows me will not walk in darkness, but will have the light of life.'

Prayer of Adoration and Confession

O God of Light, you call us into the brightness of your presence. Your love surrounds us like the warmth of the sun, and like sunshine your peace fills our hearts with joy. You are the Light of the world. We praise you.

O God of Light, you call us to live in your light, and to follow you day by day, holding each thought and word to the light of your truth, so that we may be truth; holding each word and deed to the light of your love, so that we may be love. You are the Light of the world. We praise you.

O God of Light, we live in awe of your purity, for we know that we are not always generous, loving and kind. We fail to do what is good, we are reluctant to do what is right. We grumble about the demands made on us by others, and we question your ways.

Forgive us, O God, our luke-warm worship and half-hearted service. Fire us with your zeal, your compassion, your mercy, that we may be your light in the world.   **Amen**

Prayer of Thanksgiving

Leader: For the sunshine that surrounds us:
Congregation: **We give you thanks and praise**.
Leader: For the candle flame that comforts us:
Congregation: **We give you thanks and praise**.
Leader: For the fire that warms and protects us:
Congregation: **We give you thanks and praise**.

Leader: For the strengthening of the Spirit,
surrounding us like sunshine, comforting us in the darkness,
guarding us from cold and danger:
Congregation: **We give you thanks and praise**.

Prayer of Dedication and Intercession

O Living God, we pray for your church: for those who help us
understand your teaching; for those who encourage us by their
example; for those who support us through kindness and prayer.
L: O God of Life: R: **May we be light in the world**.

O Living God, we pray for the nations: for those who lead and
must make difficult decisions; for those who speak out for the
truth; for those who serve other people.
L: O God of Life: R: **May we be light in the world**.

O Living God, we pray for our community: for those who are
sick or anxious; for those who give of their time and energy; for
those who carry the burdens of others.
L: O God of Life: R: **May we be light in the world**.

O Living God, we are the fruit of your grace and the work of
your hands. We live in your light, and minister only through your
power at work in us. Receive our offering of praise, that your light
may shine through us, this day and forever.
L: O God of Life: R: **May we be light in the world**.

Dismissal

Go into God's world,
to shine as those who live in the sunshine of God's love,
radiating goodness and persistent grace.

4th Sunday after Pentecost

Presentation

With the congregation, draw up a list of God's gifts to us. Use this as the basis for prayers of thanksgiving. Illustrate God's generosity with images of abundant giving (e.g. John 2.1–11; 6.4–14).

Call to worship

Psalm 92.1–4 or Isa. 55.1–2 or II Cor. 8.9

Prayer of Adoration

Creator God, you have poured out your love on all creation, delighting in its vastness, rejoicing in its tiny details, and in the midst of it all, you have made us in your image, to be your friends and your children. We adore you.

Saviour God, you have poured out your love on all people, delighting in our variety, rejoicing in our creativity, and in the midst of it all, you have given your life for us, rising from death to be our life forever. We adore you.

Companion God, you have poured out your love in all living, delighting in experiment, rejoicing in fulfilment, and in the midst of it all, you are alive in each one of us, empowering us to become the best that we can be. We adore you.

Prayer of Confession

Forgive us, loving God, that we have not followed your example of generosity. We have been mean in spirit, too concerned for our rights. We have sometimes shared our money, but we have so rarely shared ourselves. Accept us as we turn to you again, humble and repentant, and fill us with your grace, that we may open our hands, our hearts and our prayers to those around us day by day. **Amen**

Prayer of Intercession

Generous God, in your overflowing care, you yearn for each human being to become whole and holy, mature and fulfilled, knowing themselves to be utterly and uniquely loved. And so we pray:
– for all those who do not feel themselves to be worth anything and for those who reach out to them in their desolation,
– for those who feel isolated and for those who reach out to them in their loneliness,
– for those who feel that they have nothing to contribute and for those who reach out to them in their need,
– for all those who despair of life and for those who would love them,
– for all those who cannot accept comfort and for those who would encourage them,
– for all those who believe themselves to be beyond your saving love, and for those who would tell them the good news.
Generous God, teach us to become bearers of your peace to those in pain, this day and forever.   **Amen**

Offering Prayer

O God of all life, you have given us all things. We offer to you tokens of our gratitude, signs of our commitment, rejoicing in your steadfast love, praying for your kingdom come.

Dismissal

Go into the abundant life of God the Creator, the faithful compassion of God the Son, and the overflowing grace of God the Spirit, and know yourselves held in the generosity of God, this day and always.   **Amen**

5th Sunday after Pentecost

Presentation

A baby in the congregation could focus thoughts of God's continuing care. If this cannot be arranged, try flowers and a display of bird pictures.

Call to Worship

Do not worry about your life, what you will eat, or what you will drink, or what you you will wear ... strive first for the kingdom of God and his righteousness.

Meditation

'I remember' she said, 'holding my baby for the first time.
　For nine months a part of me,
　fed and nourished by my body,
　now an individual, alone, apart, separate,
　– and yet, for ever, a part of me.
This must be how God feels about me.'

'I remember' she said, 'holding my baby to the breast.
　Watching as the milk was sucked out,
　giving nourishment, immunity from disease,
　feeling my very self providing
　that new life and energy.
This must be how God feels about me.'

'I remember' she said, 'watching helplessly,
　when colic tensed the tiny body,
　causing pain and distress,
　anger and fear in those questioning eyes,
　– holding, watching, loving.
This must be how God feels about me.'

'I remember' she said, 'how quickly maturity came.
　No more nursing, but a gradual growth
　into joyful independence.
　And yet, forever, the bond unbroken

binding us together in love and trust.
This must be how God feels about me.'

Prayers of Intercession

We pray for those in positions of responsibility in the church
(names of Methodist and ecumenical leaders). Give them the
assurance of your presence, and confidence in moving ahead.

We pray for the countries where there is destruction and war
(names) where ideology and nationalism pervert justice and thwart
peace. Strengthen those who strive for justice, righteousness and
peace.

We pray for those who feel the tension between the claims of God
and mammon in their work and relationships. Uphold those who
are anxious because they lack money, or security, and can see no
hope on the horizon.

We pray for those who give generously of themselves in building
up their community, in local government and in community
endeavours, and sometimes feel under-valued by others. Renew
their vision and their enthusiasm. *(Where appropriate, name any
such who are linked to the local church.)*

We remember with gratitude those who have died in the faith, and
especially those who have encouraged us in our Christian
pilgrimage, and empowered us by their example. So may we work
and pray for the establishment of your kingdom, that we may, with
them, share its fullness.
Our prayers we ask in the name of Jesus.   **Amen**

Offering Prayer

Take our money, our actions, our imagination, our humanity, to be
used in the work of your kingdom.   **Amen**

6th Sunday after Pentecost

Presentation

An opportunity to use silence to show that prayer is more than words. Provide symbols – a cross, icon, banner, candle, or flowers to look at; or small objects for people to hold (during a time of prayer). Music can help – but should not crowd out all the silence.

Call to Worship

For everyone who asks receives, those who seek find, and to those who knock the door is opened.

Prayer of Praise and Thanksgiving

Almighty God, Creator of the Universe,
your power is beyond our understanding.
Faithful God, you always love us.
Accessible God, you have given us language and silence,
thoughts and emotions, and taught us how to pray.
Enabling God, help us to realize your presence with us
and to respond in Jesus' name.   **Amen**

Prayer of Confession

Forgive us for using words lightly or carelessly,
    treating people casually and without respect,
    neglecting to listen when we pray.
We confess our sins, and ask your forgiveness.   *Silence*
L: God forgives our sins and offers us new opportunities of discipleship:
R: **Thanks be to God**.

Offering Prayer

Loving God, take our money and our prayers
    our words and our silence
    our time and our talents
and use them to build your kingdom.   **Amen**

Petition and a Time of Silent Prayer

In a short introduction, explain that certain objects will provide a focus for a brief prayer, followed by a time of silence for people to use as they wish.

We bring our prayers for those: *Display the symbol of light.*
   whose lives are a light to others,
   who light candles of hope in a dark world,
   who feel their hold on Christ's light is tenuous,
   whose earthly light will soon be extinguished.   *Silence*

We bring our prayers for those: *Display the flowers*
   who bring beauty and colour to the world,
   artists, architects, cooks, carpenters and designers,
   those whose creativity and vulnerability enables others to be
   open and honest.   *Silence*

We bring our prayers for those: *Display the icon/picture.*
   who help us see God,
   who share timeless truths,
   who bring the gospel alive for us today.   *Silence*

We bring our prayers for those: *Display the cross.*
   who suffer,
   who watch others suffer,
   who are bereaved.   *Silence*

We commend all those for whom we have prayed, and ourselves, to your mercy and protection.   **Amen**

Dismissal

Go with confidence, for God will take care of you.
Go with joy, for Jesus shared your experiences.
Go in the power of the Holy Spirit who lives in you.

7th Sunday after Pentecost

Presentation

Visual display of trees with healthy/unhealthy fruit. Give everyone something to grow – an apple seed or crocus bulb, perhaps.

Call to Worship

Thus says the Lord of hosts, the God of Israel: 'Amend your ways and your doings, and let me dwell with you in this place.'

Prayer of Adoration and Confession

Almighty God, source of all that is good,
                all that is just,
                all that is true,
we bring to you, in penitence, the memories of times when our behaviour has been unworthy,
our actions unjust,
and our speech untruthful.
By the power of the Holy Spirit:
Amend our ways and our doings, and be with us in this place.

All-merciful God, from whom freedom comes,
                you defend the weak,
                you make peace to grow and flourish,
we bring to you, in penitence, the memories of times when
we have inhibited the freedom of others,
we have taken advantage of the weak,
and we have neither made nor kept the peace.
By the power of the Holy Spirit:
Amend our ways and our doings, and be with us in this place.

Meditation and Prayer of Thanksgiving

An apple seed, taken from the core of an apple – not much sign of
life there. Planted in a plastic pot, out of curiosity, really, not
expecting growth, but nothing to lose. Put on one side, forgotten …
'What's in this plant pot?' 'A weed, I expect.' 'Didn't you plant
something back in the spring?' 'I don't remember, – oh yes, I put
in an apple seed.'
Despite all the odds, the apple seedling grew, was transplanted into
the garden, and brought forth good fruit.
Dear God, thank you for having more faith in me, than I had in the
apple seed. Thank you for believing I deserved better than an
expendable cheap plastic pot. Thank you for not forgetting me, but
giving me all I need for nurture and growth. Thank you for
enabling me, through your grace, to bring forth good fruit. Help me
always to remember you are the source of goodness and growth,
for Jesus' sake.

Prayer of Intercession   *Allow plenty of silence between the suggestions for prayers.*

Loving God, we bring you our prayers for:
The underprivileged and the overprivileged,
the oppressed and the oppressors,
those who suffer in war and those who endeavour to bring peace,
those who use Jesus' name lightly, or for the wrong reasons,
those who do new things and those who follow routine,
those who face illness, bereavement, loneliness or anxiety,
ourselves, that our words and actions may be signs of our living
   faith, that others may want to follow Christ.   **Amen**

Dismissal

Go with the power of God to do his will,
Go with the sensitivity of the Holy Spirit to hear God's word,
Go with the love of Christ to live the good news.

8th Sunday after Pentecost

Presentation

Two or three people briefly give testimonies (tell stories) of their experience of God's love in a desperate situation. Or provide a visual display of life-giving situations – water, health, response to 999 calls.

Call to Worship

God says:
Those who are not my people I will call my people.

Prayer of Adoration

Caring God,
when we are sad, you open our eyes to your love for us,
You give us people who share our concerns and kindle our faith.
Caring God, we praise you and gladly accept your gifts.

Generous God,
when we try to justify our selfishness and self-righteousness, you
overwhelm us with your goodness and forgiveness.
Generous God, we praise you and gladly accept your gifts.

Powerful God,
when we remember that you have made us your people, we can
only kneel before you in awe and wonder.
Powerful God, we praise you and gladly accept your gifts.

Prayer of Confession

From your generosity, we turn to our pettiness, and ask your
forgiveness, O God.
From your love which includes the whole world, we remember
with shame that so often we exclude others from our lives, our
concern, and our prayers.
But we know that you are generous with your forgiveness, and so
we ask for it and accept it now.

We ask too, that you will help us listen to what you are saying to each of us today, and to respond, in the strength of Jesus Christ.

Prayer of Intercession

Loving God
We pray for the refugees, the stateless, those forced from their homeland. In their uncertainty about the future, in the seeming hopelessness, be their comfort. Strengthen those who work with refugees and those who are homeless, to provide security, justice and dignity.

We pray for those who are too settled and secure, and refuse to face up to the demands of the Christian pilgrimage. Strengthen those who challenge others to follow Christ wherever that may lead.

We pray for those who fear the death of loved ones in situations of war, famine, disease or illness. Uphold all who watch, and those who themselves face death – with fear, or with hope. Encourage and equip all those who bring healing and wholeness.

We pray for those who doubt your mercy and feel that they do not deserve your forgiveness. Grant them and us to accept that we are your people. Enable us to share our faith with others, and work for your inclusive kingdom.
Our prayers we ask through the name of Jesus.

Dismissal

May God be with you in the desert places
and give you hope when you are fearful,
May Jesus be with you in your daily life
and give you faith which grows and deepens,
May the Holy Spirit fill you with the assurance
of God's love for you and all humankind.   **Amen**

9th Sunday after Pentecost

Presentation

(Some years this Sunday may fall on Hiroshima Day – 6th August.)
Doves may be made of origami, after telling the story of the Japanese
girl who wanted to bring peace into the world. She encouraged
people around the world to make such paper birds, as she waited for
her own death.

Call to Worship

God has reconciled us to himself through Christ, and has given us
the ministry of reconciliation.

Prayer of Adoration and Confession

Loving God, Creator of the universe, when we look at the wonders
of the world, the mountain ranges, the silent deserts, the raging
seas, the starlit skies, we fall silent in awe and wonder.

When we consider the wonders of humankind, our agile bodies, our
complex emotions, our intelligence and understanding, we fall
silent as we remember how often we do not use our potential, and
we ask for forgiveness.

Loving God, sustainer of all you have made, you always work for
the good of your creation. As you brought order from chaos, so you
bring hope out of despair, reconciliation out of bitterness, and new
life from the old.

In silence we gratefully accept your forgiveness so readily given.
As forgiven people we renew our commitment to Jesus Christ, our
Lord.   **Amen**

Prayer of Intercession

Let us bring our prayers to God for:
those who know only how to fight,
those who insist that they alone are right,

and those who hold on to the past, because of fear or insecurity,
may they hear your words:
'Behold I make all things new.'

Those who feel that their path is the only one,
those who criticize others for being different,
and those whose minds are closed,
may they hear your words:
'Behold I make all things new.'

Those who go after any new thing,
those who want peace at any price,
those who forget that reconciliation is often painful,
and those who forget that God is the source of peace,
may they hear your words:
'Behold I make all things new.'

We pray for ourselves.
Make us receptive to listen to your word,
eager to act upon it,
and faithful to the ministry of reconciliation to which you call us,
may we hear your words:
'Behold I make all things new.'

Offering Prayer

God, you are our peace.
As we give you our gifts,
we remember that you have given us work to do, in your name.
May we listen sensitively, talk wisely, encourage lovingly, and
bring your peace.   **Amen**

Dismissal

Go willingly, in the power of the Holy Spirit, to do the work God
has given you.
You will find the unexpected, and be surprised,
you will find new strength and lose your weariness,
you will discover that God, through Christ, is making all things
new.

10th Sunday after Pentecost

Presentation

Stories of modern saints could be acted, or portrayed in song or pictures.

Call to Worship

Proclaim the good news, the kingdom of heaven has come near you. See I am sending you out like sheep in the midst of wolves. So be wise as serpents and innocent as doves.

Prayer of Adoration

God, who made the world, and everything in it, we marvel at the variety and richness, and we adore your name.

God, who continually recreates the world, forgiving and offering new opportunities, we marvel at your generosity, and we adore you.

God, who shares our experiences, both good and bad, we marvel at your faithfulness to us, and we adore you.   **Amen**

Prayer of Confession

Loving God, you spoke to us, and we did not listen.
'I am sending you', said God. We looked around to see who would go, then as realization dawned, we made off in the opposite direction.
L: So we pray: R: **Forgive us, and send us**.

'I need workers', said God. We looked around to see who would respond, then, making our excuses, we tried to tip-toe gently away.
L: So we pray: R: **Forgive us, and empower us**.

'You must be wise as serpents', said Jesus. We looked around, startled and amazed. We did not expect to bring intelligence into spreading the gospel!
L: So we pray: R: **Forgive us, and embolden us**.

'Be innocent as doves', said Jesus. We looked around at those we
must face – challenged to be accepting, gentle, peaceful.
L: So we pray: R: **Forgive us and inspire us**.

God hears our prayers and forgives our sins. **Thanks be to God**.

Prayer of Intercession and Thanksgiving

God, our Father and Mother, we pray for:
those who run away,
those who run wild,
and those who do not respond to your word.

Those who see what needs doing but do not want to be involved,
those who do not know how to be involved,
and those who cannot see what God wants them to do.

Those who use words too readily, or irresponsibly,
those who hide behind words,
and those who cannot find the right words to tell the good news.

For those who seek peace,
        keep peace,
        make peace.
We thank you for those who have spoken to us – by word and
action – of the nearness of the kingdom of heaven. In silence we
remember them …
Make us faithful to our calling, for Jesus' sake.   **Amen**

Dismissal

Go and tell others the good news of the nearness of God's
kingdom, by your words and your actions. God will be with you,
giving you courage, endurance and love.

11th Sunday after Pentecost

Presentation

Make a collage of pictures or poems showing people saying goodbye, or facing situations of danger or ridicule.

Call to Worship

The one who endures to the end will be saved.

Prayer of Adoration and Thanksgiving

Powerful God, Creator of the world, your authority and majesty are beyond our understanding. We are silent in awe and wonder at your love and care for all you have made.

Thank you for trusting us to care for the world, and to care for each other. Thank you for the friendship and example of Jesus, and for the presence of the Holy Spirit.   **Amen**

Prayer of Confession and Petition

Forgive the times when we cannot take the mockery,
Forgive the times when we cannot face the loneliness,
Forgive the times when we do not protest against injustice.
O Lord, hear our prayer. Forgive and empower us.

Forgive and transform our bitterness when decisions are hard,
Forgive and transform our self-centredness,
Forgive and transform our fear of the unknown future.
O Lord, hear our prayer. Forgive and empower us.

Share our pain when we find discipleship hard,
Share our sadness at unavoidable partings,
Share all our journeyings in your name.
O Lord, hear our prayer. Forgive and empower us.

Meditation

Though I wished the moment could last for ever, Jeremiah warned of perils ahead: exile, slavery, degradation, no place of worship. What is left, Lord, without home, country, family, faith? Can you use this pain to show what true faith is?

Though I wished the moment could last for ever, Jesus sent us out, with warnings of persecution, floggings, betrayal and hatred. Be wise, you said, Lord, innocent, unworried. Can you use such endurance to show what true faith is?

Though I wished the moment could last for ever, Paul said farewell, then went to imprisonment and probable martyrdom. When our forefathers and mothers hand the responsibility to us, may we have faith, vision, and words, through your grace.   **Amen**

Prayer of Intercession

For the exiled and the homeless,
For the rootless and the lonely,
For the anxious and the insecure:
   R: **Loving God, we pray**.
For those whose faith is tested,
For those whose faith is wavering,
For those whose faith is challenged:
   R: **Loving God, we pray**.
For those who encourage us,
For those who discourage us,
For ourselves as we face the future:
   R: **Loving God, we pray.**

Dismissal

Go in the strength of God, the all-powerful,
Go in the love of Jesus, the ever-vulnerable,
Go in the power of the Holy Spirit, and endure to the end.   **Amen**

12th Sunday after Pentecost

Gen. 24.62–67
Col. 3.18–25
Matt. 12.43–50

Presentation

The congregation is invited beforehand to bring a photograph (individual or family) attached to a postcard giving names, and a sentence about themselves. These are put up on a notice-board, to show the 'church family'.

Call to Worship

'Whatever you are doing, put your whole heart into it, as if you were doing it for the Lord.'

Prayer of Adoration and Confession

Loving God, Creator of all living things, we adore you.
Caring God, source of all love, we adore you.
Redeeming God, provider of purpose and meaning, we adore you.

For the times when we are selfish and greedy, taking for granted those we love, and those who love us:
R: **Forgive us, we pray.**

For the times when we do not enjoy and appreciate the loving relationships you have given us:
R: **Forgive us, we pray.**

For the times we do not accept the responsibilities that loving brings:
R: **Forgive us, we pray.**

For the times we forget that those who do your will are Christ's sisters and brothers, and ours too:
R: **Forgive us, we pray.**

In silence, we offer our own confession …
The Lord, hears our prayer, and forgives our sins:
R: **Amen. Thanks be to God.**

Prayer of Intercession and Petition

God of love, you have set us in families, among friends, and in
communities, that together we may learn more about you.
We pray for those closest to us:
    for those who have shown us kindness and understanding,
    who have encouraged and affirmed us,
    who have helped us to enjoy life.
Help us, through the relationships you have given us, to learn
more of you and your love.

God of mercy, we pray for:
those who feel misunderstood, discouraged and unhappy;
those who are sad or anxious because of the breakdown of
relationships;
those who mourn the death of loved ones;
those who live in countries where there is war, or internal strife.
Bring healing of memories, restoration of relationships and comfort
and peace to those who are bruised and hurt.

God of hope, you are always surprising us with new opportunities
and gifts. Help us to see Christ in those we meet and, through your
grace, may others see Christ in us.   **Amen**

Offering Prayer

Symbols are brought forward with the collection plates.

Generous God,
We offer our relationships. *Display a photograph.*
We offer our homes. *Display a children's toy house.*
We offer our activities. *Display a paintbox, etc.*
We offer our worship. *Display a service or hymn book.*
We offer our money. *Display the collection plates.*
As we commit ourselves to each other and to you.   **Amen**

Dismissal

Go with the power of the Holy Spirit,
into the world which God has made.
Go in love, to share your life with others;
Go in mercy, to care for those who need you;
Go in hope, for you join in the work of Christ.   **Amen**

13th Sunday after Pentecost

Presentation:

A display of hope overcoming despair – could be visual, with pictures, collage, photographs, or else oral, with music or poetry illustrating this theme.

Call to Worship

In hope we were saved.

Prayer of Adoration

Creating God, in hope you made the world, and it was very good.

Sustaining God, in hope you continue the work of creation, and restoration, and keep making all things good again.

Saving God, in hope you bring good out of evil, and prove that love is stronger than hate.

Prayer of Confession

Holy God, we so often fail to uphold what is good and honest, right and true. Forgive us when we fall short of the high standards we should have. Make us ready to admit our faults, grateful to receive your forgiveness, and eager to renew our commitment to live in your strength.
L: Our sins are forgiven: R: **Amen. Thanks be to God.**

Prayer of Intercession

We pray for those who suffer famine, and lack adequate food, with
  no hope of good harvest, as crops fail, and animals die;
for those who work for justice and peace, and seek to
  alleviate famine and hunger.
L: Lord, in your mercy: R: **Hear our prayer.**

We pray for those who suffer illness, anxiety, loneliness;
for doctors, nurses and others who have a caring ministry, and
   seek to bring healing and wholeness.
L: Lord, in your mercy: R: **Hear our prayer.**

We pray for those who are the victims of waste and injustice; those
who seek to care for the environment, fighting pollution, and waste;
   those who work for wise use of the world's resources.
L: Lord, in your mercy: R: **Hear our prayer**.

We pray for those who are burdened with worry and troubles;
those who long for hope and comfort in their distress;
for those who proclaim your message of good news in situations of
   despair.
L: Lord, in your mercy: R: **Hear our prayer**.

Offering Prayer

May the money we offer today,
and that which we keep to spend in other ways,
be used to your glory.

May the time we spend in prayer and meditation,
and the time we use in our many activities,
be used to your glory. **Amen**

Dismissal

Go with faith from this time of worship,
to join God at work in the world.
May hope inspire you, through difficulties and doubts,
for Jesus will be with you in all you do.
Leave here, filled with the Holy Spirit,
to share God's love with those you meet. **Amen**

14th Sunday after Pentecost

Presentation

Everyone is given a symbol of God's enduring love such as a stone or a pebble, to hold during the opening prayer.

Call to Worship

I will sing of your steadfast love, O Lord, forever; and proclaim your faithfulness to all generations.

Prayer of Adoration

God of peace, we adore you.
Still our busy-ness and make us listen.
Calm our anxieties, and help us to rest in you.
Time of silent prayer

God of the past, we adore you.
You inspired our mothers and fathers in the faith,
shared their sorrows and joys, and gave them courage.
Silence
God of the present, we adore you.
You have brought us together in this place.
Enfold us in your love, and inspire the worship we offer.
Silence
God of the future, we adore you.
Take from us all that separates us from you.
Show us your purpose for us, and enable us to walk in your way,
that at the last we may take our place in your heavenly kingdom.
Silence
Through Jesus Christ our Lord.   **Amen**

Prayer of Confession

Merciful God, forgive the sins of which we are ashamed,
    forgive the sins of which we are proud,
        forgive the sins which we do not notice,
            for your mercy's sake.
L: The Lord hears our prayer: R: **Thanks be to God**.

Prayer of Thanksgiving

Thank you for faith, given by grace,
                    nurtured by prayer,
                    increased by study.
Thank you for hope, grounded in experience,
                    enabled by memory,
                    fulfilled in practice.
Thank you for love, begun in creation,
                    developed in relationships,
                    completed in resurrection.　**Amen**

Prayer of Intercession

We pray for those who are anxious about the future; those who
have difficult decisions to make; and those who are troubled.
L: Bring your comfort and courage:
R: **God of steadfast love.**

We pray for those who are ill or unhappy; and those who face
physical, mental or emotional difficulties.
L: Bring your healing and wholeness:
R: **God of steadfast love.**

We pray for those who have grown complacent; and those whose
faith needs refreshment.
L: Bring your challenge and excitement:
R: **God of steadfast love.**

Dismissal

May the memory of God's love enfold you,
May the assurance of Christ's presence empower you,
May the joy of the Holy Spirit enable you to glimpse heaven here,
and enter it at the last.　**Amen**

15th Sunday after Pentecost

Presentation

God's people are called to live together in unity. A shared vision and harmony are what God desires for us, not competition and division. The parable of the lost sheep could be dramatized, with emphasis on the incompleteness of the flock of ninety-nine. Provide visual symbols of unity, like Ezekiel's book, to be discussed. (i.e. a string of beads, jigsaw, chain, engine, etc.)

Call to Worship

Jesus said, 'Where two or three meet together in my name,
  I am there among them.'
Come and rejoice, for Jesus is with us.
Come, let us worship together, in his name.

Prayer of Confession

Lord, we need your help
if we are to live together in unity and love.
Too often, our prejudices, fears and false pride
create divisions between us
and stop us loving one another
as we know we should.
We get upset by those
whose beliefs differ from ours
and forget our shared faith in you.
We get angry with those
whose plans for the church differ from ours
and forget to seek a shared vision.
We find it hard to get on with those
whose background differs from our own
and forget that we each belong to you.
Lord, you have no favourites.
We are all equally precious in your sight,
and you made us to depend on one another.
We ask you to forgive our petty disagreements
and the reserved nature of our love.

Teach us to respect one another, enjoy one another,
and care for one another.
Teach us to live as one body, in you.
In the name of Jesus Christ, our Lord and Saviour,
who died to break down the barriers of sin.   **Amen**

Prayer of Intercession

Let us pray for our world divided against itself – rich against poor,
religion against religion, country against country. We pray for ...
Lord, enlarge the vision of the rulers of the world, that they may
together seek justice and peace, food, education, shelter and
healthcare for all people.
L: Lord, may your kingdom come: R: **May your will be done.**

Let us pray for our community divided against itself – wealthy
against deprived, race against race, husband against wife, children
against parents. We pray for ...
Lord, enlarge our understanding of one another and our concern to
meet one another's needs, so that together we might build a society
that is harmonious and healthy, ordered, secure, nurturing and
caring.
L: Lord, may your kingdom come: R: **May your will be done.**

Let us pray for our church divided against itself – culture against
culture, denomination against denomination, theology against
theology, interest group against interest group. We pray for ...
Lord, enlarge our loving and our desire for unity, so that together
we may fulfil our calling to be the Body of Christ. Make us one,
that the world might believe.
L: Lord, may your kingdom come: R: **May your will be done.**

Dismissal

God has made you one with him in Christ Jesus.
God has made you one with one another.
Go out together in the power of the Holy Spirit,
to pray and work for a world united in love.   **Amen**

16th Sunday after Pentecost

Presentation

This Sunday we continue to look at the way in which God wants us to live together. God's forgiveness of us is inextricably linked with the forgiveness we show one another. The Genesis reading needs to be set in context and the Matthew reading would dramatize well. Thoughts on mending broken objects (with visual aids) could lead into thinking about forgiveness.

Call to Worship

We are here to worship the living God,
to offer heartfelt thanks and praise,
not because we are holy,
not because we are good,
but because we are loved, forgiven and free.

Prayer of Adoration and Confession

Eternal God,
we praise you for your steadfast love towards humankind.
You created us, provided for us, watched over us.
But although we chose to disobey you,
although we chose to sin,
although we chose to leave you,
You did not leave us.
You continued to call us and guide us,
always longing for our return.

Eternal God,
we praise you for your steadfast love towards humankind.
For speaking to us through your prophets
and offering us chance upon chance
to hear and obey your word.
For although we close our ears to you,
you do not stop speaking to us,
you continue to challenge and comfort us,
Always longing to be heard.

Eternal God,
we praise you for your steadfast love towards humankind.
For sending us your Word of Love in human form;
the undeserved gift of the life of your Son.
So, although we still disobey you,
and find it hard to follow in Christ's way,
yet we know you forgive us and will help us,
always longing to live in us,
always longing for our love.

Meditation

Lord, forgiving costs so much.
I have to swallow my pride.
I have to absorb and not return the pain.
I have to wipe away blinding tears,
so that I can see the person who wounded me,
as just another person, and not my enemy.
I have to take the time
to mend what is broken.
I have to let go of the past,
and live in today.

Lord, forgiving costs so much.
And yet it cost you more.
It cost you torturing pain.
It cost you death.
But in that death was life for us all.

Lord, forgiving costs so much.
But hatred and resentment cost even more,
for they are the wounds that fester and spread,
the wounds that lead to lasting death.

Lord, give me the strength to forgive.
In the name of your crucified Son, Jesus Christ,
my risen Redeemer and my ever-living Friend.   **Amen**

Ex. 20.1–17
Eph. 5.1–5
Matt. 19.13–30

17th Sunday after Pentecost

Presentation

*The keyword for Christian community living is 'love' – but this does
not replace moral codes of behaviour. Instead it transforms them, by
making the demand that we go beyond the external observance of
rules into relationships where we give our very selves to meet the
deepest needs of others. Ask the congregation to suggest some rules
for modern Christian living, and use these as a basis for the prayer
of confession.*

Call to Worship   *(Psalm 106)*

It is good to give thanks to the Lord,
    for his love endures for ever.
Who can tell of the Lord's mighty acts
    and make all his praises heard?
Happy are they who act justly
    and do what is right at all times!

Prayer of Adoration

It takes love to make a world out of nothing.
It takes love to take big risks,
to make woman and man.
It takes love to give humankind the freedom,
to love or not to love.
Parent God, we praise you for your creative love.

It takes love to enter a world with nothing.
It takes love to take big risks,
to become human.
It takes love to give yourself to others,
to be loved or not to be loved.
Incarnate God, we praise you for your saving love.

It takes love to live by God and nothing else.
It takes love to take big risks,
to make the leap of faith.
It takes love to offer yourself to others
to be loved or not to be loved.

God within us, we praise you for your strengthening love.

God the Creator, God the Savour, God the Sustainer, we worship and adore you for the glory of your love.   **Amen**

Prayer of Confession

Loving Father God, we are sorry that we have/have not ...

L: Father, we have not loved our neighbours as ourselves:
R: **Father, forgive us**. *To be repeated each time.*

Lord, we cannot save ourselves from our sins.
But with you all things are possible.
Lord, forgive us and save us,
in the name of your Son, Jesus Christ,
who, for love of us, gave up his life,
that we might know ourselves forgiven.   **Amen**

Offering Prayer

Lord, you have shown us
that to love means to give,
even at great cost to ourselves.
Accept these gifts of money
as a small part of our offering to you,
as a small part of our offering of love.   **Amen**

Dismissal and Blessing

God has given you life.
God has given you love.
God has given you faith.
Go and live your life for God, share your love with those around you, and spread the good news of Jesus Christ.
And the rich blessing of God, Creator, Saviour and Sustainer, go with you.   **Amen**

18th Sunday after Pentecost

Presentation

We need to work to eat; A simple fact of life that becomes more complex in a more complex society. The readings tell us of our responsibility to provide for ourselves, and the enjoyment we can have from the fruits of our labour. The Gospel reminds us that we all need an income, but that God is concerned that we all have what we need, even if this does not seem 'fair'. We can celebrate work – what does their work mean to members of the congregation? But we should also ask – what is the difference between needs and wants? Mime or dance to vv.3–8 of the Ecclesiastes reading.

Call to Worship

There is a time for work, a time for rest, a time for play.
This is our time to worship God,
to come together and pray.
This is our time to listen to God's word,
so we may work for him, rest in him,
and enjoy the life he gives us.

Meditation

Work – sometimes I give it too much importance.
I spend too much time on it,
to the detriment of my relationships, my well-being,
my spiritual growth.
Sometimes I put too much emphasis on work,
asking people what they do,
rather than finding out who they are.
Sometimes I eat myself up with worry about work
and lose my perspective on life,
lose all sense of enjoyment.
Lord, help me to see that work does not always have to come first.
Help me to get my priorities right.

Work – sometimes I give it too little importance.
I give too little thought to those unable to work,
to their feelings and problems.

I put too little of myself into what I do,
and so derive no satisfaction from helping others.
I put too little of you, Lord, into my daily life,
content to be a Sunday Christian.

Lord, help me to see that work enriches human life, and that all I
do should be done for you. Forgive my selfishness and narrowness
of vision, in the name of your Son, Jesus Christ, who showed us
what true human life can be.   **Amen**

Offering Prayer

Money used to pay for work done.
Money used to buy what we need.
Lord, take this offering of our money and use it,
that your work may be done in the world,
and your love reach those in need.   **Amen**

Prayers of Intercession

Let us pray for humankind, as people labour to provide for
themselves, their families, their communities:
We pray for those who, no matter how hard they work, have too
little to live on.   *Silence*
We pray for those who gain great wealth from their work, and carry
a heavy responsibility to use it well.   *Silence*
We pray for those who have no work, who feel deprived and
belittled.   *Silence*
We pray for those in charge of other workers, who have delicate
relationships to maintain.   *Silence*
We pray for those who have retired, who seek a new direction for
their lives.   *Silence*
We pray for those who are just starting work, full of excitement
and apprehension.   *Silence*
We make our prayers in the name of Jesus Christ, the carpenter,
teacher and healer who is Lord of all.   **Amen**

Josh. 6.1–20
Heb. 11.17–22, 29–31
Matt. 21.18–37

19th Sunday after Pentecost

Presentation

The readings today are full of drama – faith can have very dramatic consequences. We need to be trustfully daring to let God have full rein in our lives. We will then be amazed by what God can do through us.

There are many stories of people overcoming tremendous obstacles with God's help. There may be members of the congregation willing to give suitable, brief testimonies.

Call to Worship   (*Psalm 117*)

Praise the Lord, all nations! Extol him, all you peoples!
For his love protecting us is strong,
the Lord's faithfulness is everlasting.
Praise the Lord.

Prayer of Adoration

Lord, what marvellous things have been done
by those who put their faith in you!
Walls have been brought tumbling down:
walls of hatred and suspicion,
   of prejudice and indifference.
Mountains have been moved:
mountains of apathy and despair,
   of cynicism and doubt.
Lord, what marvellous things have been done
by those who put their trust in you!

Lord, what marvellous things you do
in the lives of those who put their trust in you:
changing old ways of thinking;
creating new ways of living;
revealing the transforming power of your love,
the love that builds up and binds together.
Lord, what marvellous things you do
in the lives of those who put their trust in you!

Almighty God, you revealed yourself to us in Jesus Christ
as a God who loves us to the uttermost,
who will never let us go,
a God who is faithful to his children,
a God whom we can trust with our lives.
We thank and praise you for always being there for us,
ready to receive us when we leap into your arms;
overjoyed to accept us as we are
and to be invited to help us to be what we can be.
Faithful and trustworthy God,
we thank and praise you.   **Amen**

Prayer of Petition

I need more faith, Lord.
I believe in you, but I get scared
of the demands I think you might make
if I give myself wholly to you.
I need more faith, Lord,
not because I long to do miracles
but because I am afraid to open myself up
to other people and to you.
I need more faith, Lord,
for when the times of testing come,
times of sorrow, pain, anxiety,
times when your strength alone will do.
I need more faith, Lord,
to live life boldly and to the full,
to know the depths and heights of love,
to know you.

Lord, in my little faith, I pray to receive more.
Lord, hear my prayer.   **Amen**

Dismissal

God calls you to live by faith in him.
Your faith will guide you, inspire you, support you.
Go out into the world in faith.

20th Sunday after Pentecost

Presentation

The theme of 'authority' needs sensitive handling. Is 'authority' vested in the government, parliament, the police, school teachers ...? Thinking how rules such as the 'Highway Code' keep people safe is one way of explaining the value of rules in society. Following God's rules is the best way to run a family, community or country.

Call to Worship

Love your neighbour as yourself. Love the Lord your God.
We worship God who loves us and inspires our love for others.

Prayer of Adoration

We praise you, wonderful God, for your wisdom.
You have given us laws for life,
    which are set out for the good of all.
You have given us your love for life,
    so that we may enjoy life in all its fullness.
Your wisdom is wiser than ours,
    your laws greater than any human law,
    your love stronger than any human love.
In Jesus you have set us a supreme example to follow,
by the Spirit you have given us the strength to obey.
Creator God, may our lives be lived in righteousness
    as an example to all.   **Amen**

Prayer of Confession

Great God, we know that a righteous life is not just a matter of obeying the right rules, following the laws of the land.
A godly life means we have to love you and love our neighbours.
We ask for your forgiveness
    for the many times we have broken your commands:
    when we have put ourselves before others,
    when we have followed our own way and not yours,
    when our love for others has been feeble,
    and we have not expressed our love for you.

Forgive us, renew us, fill us with your Spirit,
so that we can live under your authority
and acknowledge you as the only Lord of our lives.
Then everyone will say 'what a wise and understanding people the
church is!' and come to know you as the Lord their God.   **Amen**

Offering Prayer

We render this money to God in gratitude for all we have received.
Lord, take these coins of the realm, marked with the head of the
Queen, and use them to spread the realm of your holy kingdom.
Amen

Prayers of Intercession   *A framework and response*

We pray for those who hold authority in nations,
thinking especially about … (*world leaders, United Nations, etc.*)
L: Lord God, whose authority is over all: R: **Give wisdom to us.**
We pray for those who hold authority in our country,
thinking especially about … (*government, employers, judiciary,
etc.*)
L: Lord God, whose authority is over all: R: **Give wisdom to us.**
We pray for those who hold authority in our community,
thinking especially about … (*police, local councillors, etc.*)
L: Lord God, whose authority is over all: R: **Give wisdom to us.**
We pray for those whose lives are under the authority of God,
thinking especially about … (*ministers, preachers, etc.*)
L: Lord God, whose authority is over all: R: **Give wisdom to us.**

Wise God,
we are constantly amazed by the example set for us by Jesus.
May we seek to follow his words and ways so that we can
live together in peace and harmony under your benevolent
authority.   **Amen**

Dismissal

You are God's and belong to God alone.
Go under the authority of God and live your lives by the inspiration
of the Spirit according to his wise and holy ways,
and may God's holy blessing be upon you, now and
forever.   **Amen**

21st Sunday after Pentecost

Presentation

The parable of the talents is paired with a reading which is also about using our God-given gifts but like the parable is also about preparing to meet God at the end of time. The parable can easily be dramatized but careful consideration needs to be given to the end of the story if children are present.

Call to Worship   (*I Peter 4.11*)

In all things let God be glorified through Jesus Christ;
to him belong glory and power for ever.   Amen.

Prayer of Confession

So much has been given, so little has been used.
Generous God, we know that you have given us so many riches:
wealth, skills, love and life itself;
and it is with sadness and sorrow that we have to admit
that we have not used these gifts for your glory
but selfishly for our own ends.
We have wasted money on idle pursuits,
　　neither using it creatively to increase its value
　　nor supplying the needs of others.
We have squandered our talents,
　　not recognizing that they are from you
　　and keeping them to ourselves.
We have been jealous and greedy for love,
　　neither giving as much as we received
　　nor sharing it with the unloved.
We have been self-centred,
　　not understanding life as a gift from you
　　and hiding away the hope of eternal life.
Forgive our foolish ways, fill us with all that is good, and
make us courageous in using your gifts to your glory.   **Amen**

Meditation of Thanksgiving and Dedication

Do I give you joy, Lord?
You have entrusted me with small things, talents and skills:
some I know and practise, some I hardly understand,
some I keep hidden away.
I know these things give me joy,
I like it when people praise me for doing things well,
I like it when someone appreciates my help,
I enjoy it when I say the right thing –
then I bask in glory because I am liked, loved.
But do I give you joy?
Do I use all the gifts which your generous nature has bestowed?
If I have five measures, do I give five more in return?
Or do I keep a bit back, hold some in reserve, not letting
on what I can do, afraid of being open and giving freely.
I thank you for what I have received.
Give me wisdom to use these talents,
in work, through the church, in your service,
so that I give you glory, and my life reflects your love.
You promised: to those who have shall more be given.
Give me more, and I will give you even greater joy.

Offering Prayer

Master, you have entrusted us with so much,
every penny we have is because you have given us talents for
work: wisdom, strength, initiative, imagination, kindness, love.
We offer to you what we have been given and pray that through the
church this money will help many more to come to know and love
you, and so your kingdom will increase.   **Amen**

Blessing

May the Lord bless you with every good gift. Inspired by the
Spirit, use your talents to proclaim him to the world.
And when the time comes to meet God face to face, you will be
able to stand before him and will receive the gift of eternal life.

Isa. 45.14–25
Acts 15.1–2, 22–29
Matt. 26.6–13

22nd Sunday after Pentecost

Presentation

*It is hard to see the connection between these readings, but perhaps
the theme of acceptance links them together. The Matthew reading is
the most appropriate for all-age worship. The call to worship and the
Gospel reading could be dramatized or mimed.*

Call to Worship

Lord, we fall at your feet,
bowing ourselves in worship,
pouring out our love in praise and prayer.
Do not reject our offering
but embrace us with your love.

Prayer of Adoration

Generous God,
we cannot fully understand the immensity of what you have done
for us, in sending your Son, Jesus, into the world.
For his teaching and example,
Lord: **We pour at your feet our praise and adoration.**
For his care for the sick and poor,
Lord: **We pour at your feet our praise and adoration.**
For his obedience, even to death on the cross,
Lord: **We pour at your feet our praise and adoration.**
For his forgiveness,
Lord: **We pour at your feet our praise and adoration.**
For his opening the way to eternal life,
Lord: **We pour at your feet our praise and adoration.   Amen**

Prayer of Confession

It is so easy to be critical,
    especially of those who don't do as we do,
    speak with the words we use,
    or act in a manner we would not choose.
Forgiving God, you understand and forgive us when we make
mistakes,
help us to be understanding to all your people.   **Amen**

Meditation   *After Matthew reading*

The disciples didn't know what was to happen,
   but the woman knew and was prepared.
The disciples worried about the money,
   but the woman was concerned only with her Lord.
The disciples wanted everything to be right,
   but the woman only wanted Jesus to be anointed.
The disciples are remembered,
   but an unknown woman is remembered too.
May our small acts of love not go unnoticed by you, Lord,
as we strive to be good disciples.
May our chief concern be not ourselves,
but only to worship and serve you.

Offering Prayer

Generous God,
we need money to live,
to meet the cost of living.
But the cost of true life is more than money.
The cost of true life demands that everything
that we possess, that we do, that we are,
is poured out extravagantly at your feet.   **Amen**

Prayer of Petition

The way to you, loving God, is open.
You do not demand we mark our body.
You do not require us to follow petty rules.
You do not need us to fulfil certain actions.
You do not expect sacrificial offerings.
You do not seek conformity to one understanding.
You do not want us to accept only one race.
You ask nothing,
except that we love you and love our neighbours,
and we shall know your undeserved love.   **Amen**

Blessing

Go in peace,
devote your lives to serving God.
The blessing of God be upon you,
today and forever.   **Amen**

Last Sunday after Pentecost

Presentation

The obvious theme is 'the Last Day', with three pictures of heaven. Make a list of what the congregation would like to see and not see in heaven i.e. love, peace, joy, / tears, crime, hate etc. These could form the basis for a prayer of intercession (see below). The Matthew reading could easily be mimed, perhaps updated to have batteries in torches rather than oil lamps.

Call to Worship   *(Rev. 7.12) Using different voices*

Amen! Praise and glory and wisdom, thanksgiving and honour, power and might, be to our God for ever!   **Amen**

Prayer of Adoration

When we look back in time we praise you, God of the past;
    for the creation of the universe, the stars, the sun and the earth,
    the care of the people of Israel, rescuing them from slavery,
    the commandments given to Moses to guide the Jews,
    the words of the prophets giving encouragement and challenge,
    the great gift of Jesus, his example and teaching,
    his death which brings forgiveness,
    his rising again which opened the way to eternal life,
    the gift of the Spirit, inspiring and comforting the disciples,
    the many Christians who have passed on the good news of
Christ.

When we look around us we praise you, God of the present;
    for the beauty of the world, its colour and vitality,
    the fellowship of the church, caring for each other,
    the guidance of the Bible,
    the words of preachers and teachers encouraging us,
    the presence of Jesus, alive in the church,
    the empty cross signifying his gift of salvation,
    the promise of heaven for those who have died in faith,
    the Spirit which enables us to work and witness for Jesus,
    the world-wide church still growing and serving Christ.

When we look ahead we praise you, God of the future;
   for the new heaven and new earth revealed to John the Divine,
   the fellowship of the saints, united in the love of God,
   the knowledge that all wisdom will be revealed to us,
   the words which promise a better time ahead,
   meeting Jesus face to face
   forgiveness from sin and salvation for souls,
   a place in heaven united with God,
   the surrounding love of the Spirit,
   united with the saints and angels
         and praising you for ever and ever. **Amen**

Prayer of Intercession   *Collect ideas of opposites*

We live in a world torn apart by war,
   but you promise us the peace of heaven.
We live in a world of grief and tears,
   but you promise us the consolation of heaven.
We live in a world of bereavement and death,
   but you promise us the comfort and new life of heaven.
We live in a society ruined by crime and greed,
   but you promise us a heaven of sharing and equality.
We live in a society filled with hate,
   but you promise us a place in heaven surrounded by love. *etc.*
Lord of heaven and earth,
   we look forward, at the end of our days,
   to being with you in heaven.
Until that time comes
   enable us to play our part in creating heaven on earth,
   knowing that we are already living in your kingdom,
   under your authority and your love.
May your kingdom come, your will be done,
   for ever and ever. **Amen**

Blessing

Be always ready to meet the Bridegroom, Jesus Christ,
wait in hope, wait with patience, wait in love,
and be blessed with the grace of our Lord Jesus Christ,
the love of God, and the fellowship of the Holy Spirit, today and
forever. **Amen**

Church Anniversary

Presentation

The readings are about various ways in which we meet God, and the need for the church to offer such opportunities. We hold the anniversary of a church building in that context. Ask two or three people to say briefly how the church has been a place where they have known God's presence. Even quite young children can have something helpful to say if they are allowed to use their own words.

Call to Worship *(Adapted from Heb. 10.22–4)*

As we worship,
let us be sincere in heart,
   filled with faith,
   and concerned for one another.

Prayer of Adoration

Wonderful and loving God,
you deserve all the praise our mouths can sound,
         all the love our hearts contain,
         all the obedience our lives can show.
We come seeking you, but you are already here,
waiting to bless us with your love.
Sometimes you meet us in unexpected ways and in unexpected
places, surprising us with your hidden care.
You watch over us at all times,
in our waking and in our sleeping.
In Jesus Christ your Son you have made known to us
your way of perfect love.
Constant and never-changing God,
we offer you our adoration.   **Amen**

Prayer of Thanksgiving

O Lord our God,
We thank you for:
– those of past generations who have worshipped you here,
– those who in this place, have taught the Christian faith to others,
– those whose ministries have been a source of blessing in this
  church,

– those who have faithfully borne responsibilities in this
  congregation.
We thank you for:
– those who minister to us, especially for … our minister (*and
  his/her family*)
– those who bear office in this church
– those who look after the organizations and fellowship groups
– those who contribute to our worship week by week.
We thank you for:
– being here together in worship,
– for the story of your love which we hear from the Bible,
– for the sacraments of Baptism and Holy Communion,
– for those special moments when we are sure of your presence.
Through Jesus Christ our Lord.   **Amen**

Prayer of Intercession

Let us pray for:
>The life and witness of this congregation in the neighbourhood in
>which God has set us; for our fellow Christians in other churches
>in this neighbourhood, and for the other churches in our circuit.

Lord, may the life of our churches be a way in which people can
meet you, and come to know your love in Jesus Christ.

Let us pray for:
>Those who may have felt unwelcomed by the church; for any
>whose involvement with the church has brought too much pain
>and too little joy, and for any who once came to worship, but no
>longer do so.

Lord, make us ever eager to welcome the lost and the rejected, that
wounds may be bound up and your peace may be shared.

Let us pray for:
>Those amongst whom we live and work; the lonely and the
>bewildered, the hurt and the neglected, the housebound and the
>handicapped, the despairing and the frightened.

Lord, open our eyes to the needs which are all around us, and help
us to be a church which serves the needs of others. Through Christ
our Lord.   **Amen**

Harvest Festival

Gen. 8.15–22
Gal. 6.7–10
Matt. 6.25–34

Presentation

There will be many local traditions to observe today. While it is right that our Harvest celebrations should take account of poverty and injustice in the world, make sure that the main emphasis is on thankfulness for God's creating and sustaining love.

Call to Worship

Consider how the lilies grow in the fields.
Even Solomon in all his glory
was not dressed like one of them.
If God so clothes the grass in the fields,
will he not all the more clothe you?

Prayer of Adoration

Eternal God, creator of the universe,
how glorious is your name in all the earth!
When we look up at the heavens,
made by your hands,
at the moon and stars which you have set in place,
what are we, frail human beings,
that you should care for us
and take notice of us?
Yet you have made us little less than yourself
and crowned us with glory and honour.
Eternal God, creator of the universe,
how glorious is your name in all the earth!   **Amen**

Prayer of Confession

God of love and truth and beauty,
you are our creator
and everything we have comes from you.
We confess with shame
that we have not been as grateful as we should have been
for food and clothes and comfort.

We have not been as careful as we should have been
to care for the world in which we live.
We have not been as generous as we should have been
in sharing what we have with others who have less.
Forgive us, we pray, our ingratitude,
our folly and our selfishness.
May we know that you love and accept us
and that you have forgiven our sins;
through Jesus Christ our Lord.   **Amen**

Prayer of Thanksgiving

God, whose goodness never fails,
we thank you for your generous love.
For the good and fruitful earth
and the food which we eat day by day.
L: With grateful hearts: R: **We thank you, God.**
For those who work to supply our food,
to grow and harvest crops and transport them to the shops.
L: With grateful hearts: R: **We thank you, God.**
For the greatest of all your gifts,
our Lord and Saviour Jesus Christ,
who lived and died and was raised again
to bring us life and joy.
L: With grateful hearts: R: **We thank you, God.**
For the work of your Holy Spirit
and your new creation, the church.
L: With grateful hearts: R: **We thank you, God.**
Through Jesus Christ our Lord.   **Amen**

Dismissal and Blessing

Be faithful stewards of creation.
Be grateful servants of God.
And the blessing ...

Material for Year B

9th Sunday before Christmas

Presentation

God's glory can be seen not only in the creation of the world but in the creation of relationships between the Creator and humankind, between humankind and creation, and between people. 'Things of beauty' could be displayed around the church – flowers, plants, stones, etc. and pictures of wildlife, scenery and people. The Genesis 2 account of creation could be read to a mime or dance.

Call to Worship

Bless the Lord, all created things:
sing his praise and exalt him forever.

Prayer of Adoration

Creation –
an act of imagination and will,
an act of love.
You took what there was,
the dust of the ground,
cradled and moulded it in your hands,
conceived a man.
You breathed your own life into him,
made the earthly divine,
made him always your own.
Loving Parent God,
we praise you
for the gift of life to humankind.

Creation –
an act of imagination and will,
an act of love.
You caused trees to grow,
from the same dust,
to feed us with their fruit,
to feed us with their beauty.
You formed an infinite variety of living things
to keep us company on earth,

for our human imagination to name.
Loving Parent God,
we praise you,
for the beauty and bounty of creation.

Creation –
an act of imagination and will,
an act of love.
You gave the man the breath of life,
food, beauty, power over his world,
and then, made a woman.
You gave them unity in separateness.
You gave them love:
love that begets love;
love that gives purpose to humankind.
Loving parent God,
we praise you,
for giving us one another to love.   **Amen**

Prayer of Confession

Lord, we are sorry we have spoilt things.
We have spoilt the beautiful world you designed;
we have exploited it, wasted it, polluted it.
We have spoilt our relationships with other people;
we have been selfish, uncaring and unkind.
We have spoilt ourselves;
we have smothered your life within us and turned away from you.
Lord, we are sorry we have spoilt things.
Put us right with you and with one another,
so that all together we may strive to make our world
the glorious creation you intended.   **Amen**

Dismissal

The world is your home – go out and live in it.
Its people are your family – go out in love.
Its Creator is your loving God – go out in faith and joy.

8th Sunday before Christmas

Presentation

The Genesis story is not easy to understand, but the message of the three readings is clear – evil deeds result from a broken relationship with God. The Genesis account lends itself to drama or mime. Find and cut out newspaper headlines reflecting human evil. These will then be placed at the foot of the cross during the prayer of confession.

Call to Worship

If you would find true love;
if you would know lasting joy;
if you seek truth, goodness and peace,
come to the Living God.

Prayer of Confession

Listen to what is happening in God's world:
The newspaper headlines are read by various voices.

Lord, these offerings are not acceptable to you.
The harvest of human evil, the first fruits of suffering
are not pleasing in your sight.
Lord, we confess to you
the sins of humankind,
and our sins, too:
   the sins of pride and jealousy;
   the sins of selfishness and greed;
every sin that sets ourselves up as gods
and reduces other people to things of little worth.
Lord, forgive us.
We lay our sins at the foot of the cross,
for you alone have the power to overcome human evil.
We open our hearts to your forgiveness,
that love might transform our lives.
In the name of Jesus Christ, our crucified Saviour.   **Amen**

Prayer of Intercession

Lord,
too many governments have turned their backs on you,
and rule without justice, or mercy, or compassion.
We pray for those they mistreat:
  because they think differently;
  because they look or act differently;
  because they seem of little importance.
We pray for those under regimes harsh with punishment
and those who go without necessities because their government is
corrupt.
L: Lord God, hear our prayer: R: **Rescue us from our sin.**

Lord,
too many in our society have turned their backs on you
and live without depth, or joy, or love.
We pray for the victims of our faithlessness:
  those who hunger because we take too much;
  those who are anxious, lonely, depressed;
  those who are belittled, abused, neglected.
We pray for those for whom life has no purpose
and for those who are consumed by hatred or greed.
L: Lord God, hear our prayer: R: **Rescue us from our sin.**

Lord,
too often we turn our backs on you,
stray from the path of love and life,
and have nothing of worth to offer you or others.
We pray for those who are the victims of our sin:
  our families and friends and those we work with;
  the people whose lives we touch in many ways.
Lord, help us to keep turning back to you.
L: Lord God, hear our prayer: R: **Rescue us from our sin.**

We make our prayers in the name of Christ, who died
because of our sin and was raised again because of your forgiving
love.   **Amen**

7th Sunday before Christmas

Presentation

*The connecting theme in the three lessons is that of Abraham –
God's promise to Abraham, Abraham's response of faith in action,
and Jesus' assurance of God's continuing relationship with his
people. Talk about the promises we make. Have visual examples of
promises on display – the words of the Covenant Service, a five
pound note, a guarantee, a baptismal certificate, etc.*

Call to Worship

There is one whose promises never fail.
There is one upon whom we can always rely:
Our God, the maker of all that is,
        our protector and our friend.
Come, let us worship the living God.

Prayer

Loving God, we praise and thank you
for your many promises to us:
the promise of the rainbow
that life would continue on earth;
the promise to Abraham
that you will take care of your faithful;
the promise of the risen Christ
that evil and death are overcome;
the promise of Christ to his followers
that he will be with us for ever.

Loving God, we praise and thank you
for your many promises to us
and for the security they bring:
hope for dark days;
courage for painful times;
joy in the midst of sorrow;
support when we feel weak and afraid.

Loving God, we praise and thank you
for your many promises to us.
Forgive us when we break
our promises to you and to one another,
for the sake of your Son, Jesus Christ,
who remained faithful to the end.   **Amen**

Meditation

Lord,
it is so easy to break things,
easier to destroy than to create.
The world is full of:
   broken promises
   broken dreams
   broken relationships
   broken hearts.

Lord,
I want to be a maker,
not a breaker.
I want to build up
and not to knock down.
Give me the grace to keep my promises,
to be faithful to myself, to others and to you.

Lord,
who let your body be broken on the tree
that we might be made whole,
create from our shattered promises
a perfect mosaic of love.

Dismissal

Wherever you go, God has promised to be.
God the Creator will watch over you.
God the Son will keep you safe.
God the Holy Spirit will give you strength.
Thanks be to God.   **Amen**

6th Sunday before Christmas

Presentation

*The Israelite slaves were too full of despair to hear Moses' word of
hope. It is despair that is the opposite of faith. These passages
promise that if we hang on to God, we will be brought safely through
our suffering. A mime or drama depicting the leading of a blind
person, the roping together of climbers, or the pulling to shore of
someone drowning could be enacted.*

Call to Worship

Where the Spirit of God is, there is freedom.
Come, let us worship God in freedom and truth.

Prayer of Adoration

God, you are our sun.
Even on our darkest days
you shine on us from behind the clouds,
giving us warmth and light.
L: Saving God: R: **We praise you.**

God, you are our map.
On our pilgrimage through life,
when we feel lost, bewildered, afraid,
you show us the way ahead.
L: Saving God: R: **We praise you.**

God, you are our shield.
As we face the wounds that life inflicts,
as we battle with sin and pain and despair,
you protect our hearts and lives.
L: Saving God: R: **We praise you.**

God, you are our lifeline.
When we can find no sure footing,
when the water is deep and cold,
we cling fast to you and are pulled safe.
L: Saving God: R: **We praise you.**

God, you are our bread and wine,
nourishment for hungry souls in the desert,
body and blood given for us
to rescue us from the slavery of sin.
L: Saving God: R: **We praise you.**

God, sun and map, shield and lifeline, bread and wine, our
protector and saviour, we give you thanks and praise.   **Amen**

Prayer of Intercession

We remember before God
those who live in the pit of despair,
asking that God will release them from their slavery.
We think of those persecuted, imprisoned or tortured because of
their beliefs;
we think of those exploited, oppressed, discriminated against by
their governments. We think of ...
L: Saving God: R: **Set your children free.**

We think of those who are destitute, hungry or homeless, with no
power to improve their lives;
we think of those who are the victims of warfare, natural disaster or
epidemic. We think of ...
L: Saving God: R: **Set your children free.**

We think of those who are ill, who have chronic diseases or
disabilities or who know they are to die;
we think of those whose lives are darkened by worry, depression or
loss. We pray for ...
L: Saving God: R: **Set your children free.**

And we pray for ourselves, bringing to God the despair we feel
when we are enslaved by the demands of others, by need, by illness
or by wrong-doing. Lord, hear our prayers and release us into the
glorious freedom of your children. In the name of our crucified and
risen Saviour.   **Amen**

5th Sunday before Christmas

Presentation

Two texts sum up the theme of the readings: 'The Lord sees into the heart' and 'But many who are first will be last, and the last first.' Dramatize the I Samuel reading. Have a display of recycled products and talk about God recycling human lives, taking what the world or individuals think of little value and making something useful and beautiful.

Call to Worship   *(could be used responsively)*

I shall bless the Lord at all times:
His praise shall be ever on my lips.
In the Lord shall I glory:
The humble will hear and be glad.
Glorify the Lord with me:
Let us exalt his name forever.

Prayer of Adoration

Loving God, you amaze us;
what we think is impossible, you make happen.
You made the world from nothing,
created Man from mud and Spirit.
You promised an old man, Abraham,
and an old barren woman, Sarah,
that their family would be as many as the stars,
    and you made it happen.
You took a raw shepherd lad
    and turned him into the greatest of kings.
You took the fiercest persecutor of the first Christians
    and turned him into a founder of the church.
You took human flesh, and the divine became one of us.
You took human suffering and death upon the cross
    and turned it into an act of love
    and an act of life victorious over sin and death.
Loving God, you amaze us;
what we think is impossible, you make happen.
Take our lives and use them

that we might do something
impossibly loving
for you.   **Amen**

Prayer of Confession

All seeing God, we confess to you
the imperfection of our vision.
We look with favour upon those
who have done well for themselves,
who are successful or well-known.
We think little of those
whose light burns more dimly
but whose small flame of love
shines faithfully in the darkness.
We look with favour upon those
whom nature has endowed with beauty or fine minds.
We think little of those
whose beauty is within,
a gentle and quiet spirit
that calms and comforts troubled lives.
We look with favour upon those
who look like us,
from the same class, or race, or church.
We think little of those
who are different,
who challenge our values, assumptions, beliefs,
whose witness to you does not speak to us.
All seeing God, forgive our blindness.
Help us to see more clearly.
Help us to see into the heart.
For the sake of your Son, Jesus Christ,
the Light of the World.   **Amen**

Dismissal

Father, you restore us. Jesus, you renew us.
Holy Spirit, you refill us with the power of love.
Send us out into the world to do great things for you.

4th Sunday before Christmas
Advent 1

Presentation

To get the sense of travelling through Advent place a large star at different points around the church. On this first Sunday place it by the church door (the opening); on successive Sundays in appropriate places around the church.

Call to Worship

Wake up! Children of the light! Watch for Jesus to come!
Wait and worship in the hope of the coming Saviour!

Advent Candle Prayer   *Read by those who light the first candle.*

On this first Sunday in Advent we begin our preparation for the celebration of Christmas, the birth of Jesus at Bethlehem.
We are like those who waited eagerly in the past: the Jews waiting for God's chosen one, Mary and Joseph expecting a child, the disciples seeking the kingdom. So we too look forward to the joy of finding God in our world and our lives.
In silence the candle is lit.
Let us pray:
Lord Jesus, who came as the light of the world,
we wait again for your coming as a baby in Bethlehem.
Still, today, we long for your justice to rule the world;
peace and harmony to replace the hatred and mistrust between nations, your marvellous light to come into dark places.
You came to save us and deliver us from our sins;
we ask for your forgiveness when we have done or said wrong things.
Lead us from darkness into the light of your kingdom,
and keep us faithful in all we do for you.   **Amen**

Offering Prayer

Make us wise, Lord, in the ways we use our treasure.
May our money not constrain our lives,
but liberate us to enjoy life and bring life to others.
May this money, offered in the name of Jesus,
for the use of your church,
be used to tell the world of your unending love.   **Amen**

Prayer of Petition

We are unprepared for the coming of Christ:
    we continue our everyday, everyway lives
    as if, God, we can manage without you
    or even as if you do not exist.
We do not expect our worship to be so exciting
    that we shall meet and greet you there,
and we do not live like faithful servants awaiting your return.
Yet your promises are clear:
    though we do not know how or when or where,
    you will return, and we need to be ready.
May we respond to your loving presence in our world,
    with minds open to your truth,
    wills open to every opportunity of service,
    and hearts open in love and praise.

Then, with all your saints on earth and in heaven,
    we shall be enabled to worship and serve you now
    and prepared, at your coming, to join you in the world to
    come. **Amen**

Responsive Prayer of Intercession (*Based on Isaiah 51*)

Great God, whose promises are true,
We pray for the leaders of the world, remembering ...:
Enlighten them with your laws.
We pray for those who suffer persecution because of their faith:
Bring your everlasting deliverance.
We pray for those who are sad or sorrowful, remembering ...:
Fill their hearts with gladness.
We acknowledge your mighty acts of salvation: from the exodus to
the cross nothing is beyond your power:
**We sing and shout for joy because you are a great God of
salvation**. **Amen**

Closing Prayer

As we leave our church today, to go out into the world,
may we shine with the light of Christ.
Let us be prepared to meet Jesus in our friends and neighbours
and share with them the Christian hope we have found in him.
In the name of God, Creator, Son and Holy Spirit, send us out
with your holy blessing to live our lives for you. **Amen**

3rd Sunday before Christmas
Advent 2

Presentation

Place the star by a Bible (on the lectern or pulpit). Display different Bibles, having asked the congregation to bring their own Bibles, particularly precious 'Family' or presentation Bibles. Ask someone to say how important their Bible is to them.

Call to Worship

We meet to hear, share and celebrate the Holy Word of God in the Bible. Let us praise God, who inspired all who wrote down these words, and inspires us as we hear them today.

Advent Candle Prayer   *Read by those who light the candles.*

In our service today we think about the word of God in the Bible. As we light this candle we remember that the Bible is a source of God's truth and our guide for living.
In silence the candles are lit.
Let us pray:
Lord, we find you in the pages of the Bible,
    and we find you in our lives.
Help us to understand the words we read
    and find in them a message for today.
We are sorry when we forget what you have told us
    and act for ourselves and not for you.
Lead us into the light and truth of the gospel
    so that we might be saved, through Jesus Christ
    our Lord.   **Amen**

Prayer of Adoration

We praise you, great God,
    for your act of creation, making life from nothing,
    for creating every variety of plant and animal,
    for raising up mountains and spreading out seas.
    for making us in your image and sustaining our lives.

We praise you, wise God,
    for your covenant made with your people,

for your guiding of Abraham, Isaac and Jacob,
for the rescue of the Israelites from slavery in Egypt,
for the preaching of the prophets and the poetry of the Psalmist.

We praise you, loving God,
for the coming of your Son Jesus,
for his humble birth, and patient life of teaching and healing,
for his death on the cross and rising from the grave,
for his ascension to heaven and continuing life.

We praise you, caring God,
for the pouring of the Spirit on the disciples,
for their gradual comprehension of your saving work,
for the missionary zeal of Paul,
for the writers of letters and the Revelation of John.

We praise you, eternal God,
for all who have passed on your words and deeds in the Bible,
for those who were inspired to record their knowledge,
for those who treasured and translated your holy word,
for those who have shared the message with us.

We praise you for the gift of the Bible,
and all it means for us today.   **Amen**

Prayer after the Bible Readings

As we have heard, help us to remember.
As we have remembered, help us to learn.
As we have learnt, help us to live.
As we live, help us to share.
May your Word be alive in us.   **Amen**

Offering Prayer

We give our money, we give our love, we give ourselves,
so that all the world may know the mighty acts of God.
We offer our gifts and pray for their use
in spreading the good news about Jesus.   **Amen**

Dismissal

Inspired by the scriptures, you are qualified and equipped
to do every kind of good deed, serving God, so that you may,
in time, win the prize awarded for a righteous life
to all who wait in love for the Lord to appear.

2nd Sunday before Christmas
Advent 3

Isa. 40.1–11
II Peter 3.8–14
Mark 1.1–8

Presentation

Preparation for Christmas can be linked with preparing for God. Life is to be lived to the full now so that all are ready to share in the joy of the day of the Lord.
Place the star by the font (for John the Baptist).

Call to Worship

Isaiah 40.3–5: Alternate phrases read by two voices
Preacher: A voice cries:
Voice 1: Clear a road through the wilderness for the Lord,
Voice 2: prepare a highway across the desert for our God.
Voice 1: Let every valley be raised,
Voice 2: every mountain and hill be brought low,
Voice 1: uneven ground be made smooth,
Voice 2: and steep places become level.
Voice 1: Then will the glory of the Lord be revealed
Voice 2: and all people together will see it.
Together: The Lord himself has spoken.

Advent Candle Prayer   *Read by those who light the candles.*

We are coming closer to Christmas Day, the celebration of the birth of God's Son Jesus. Today our third candle reminds us of John the Baptist who told people to prepare themselves to meet Jesus. He challenged people to turn away from wrong-doing and find forgiveness.
In silence the candles are lit.
Let us pray:
Loving God,
we still don't respond to the call of John the Baptist as we ought.
We say we have turned away from doing wrong
but so easily slip back into old, bad ways.
We are not good enough to be loved by you,
yet still you stand by us,
you comfort us when we are sad
and give us strength for the day ahead.
May we be challenged every day by the call of John
to live new lives, following your example.   **Amen**

Prayer of Preparation

So little time, so much to do,
will we ever be ready?
We want to be prepared for anything and everything
so that all will go well and right.
But will it make any real difference?

As we prepare for Christmas this year,
   buying presents, sending cards,
   preparing food, decorating homes,
   may we not lose sight of the Christ of Christmas.
Help us to make Jesus the focus of all we do,
   to sing of his coming in carols,
   to show his love in charity,
   to find space in our busyness to think of him.

God, you have prepared everything for us,
   sent the prophets, called us to repentance,
   entered the world as a human being,
   challenged us to follow you,
   and filled us with the Holy Spirit.
For you are a patient God,
   and you are prepared to wait for us to come to our senses
   and to let you make a real difference to our lives.
Thank you for your mercy and love;
   help us to work for your glory,
   so that others may know of your Son, and be glad,
   as we have been, to welcome you into their hearts and
   lives. **Amen**

Offering Prayer

May these gifts of money be used,
   to proclaim the good news of God's love,
   to bring comfort to the sick and bereaved,
   to call people to repentance and faith,
through the work of this church and the church in all the world,
and in the name of the Lord who came in power. **Amen**

Dismissal

Go out into the world and prepare a way for the Lord.
Speak and act in loving ways to show he is with us.
God bless you and guide you in the way of all truth and justice.

Sunday next before Christmas
Advent 4

Presentation

Use the Magnificat as an introduction to the prayers of adoration: one reader for verses 36 to 46a, gradually walking to the front of the church, and a younger woman for Mary's words in 46b to 55. Use the two 'songs' to explore the theme of thanksgiving. Place the Advent star on the organ – we give glory to God.

Call to Worship

No one is as holy as the Lord.
No one is as good as our God.
Praise the Lord in actions, music and words
for our God is worthy of all worship!

Advent Candle Prayer   *Read by those who light the candles.*

Many parents are awestruck by the gift of a child,
Ḥannah praised God for Samuel, Mary praised God for Jesus.
As we light this candle and remember Mary, the mother of Jesus,
let us praise God who gave us new life in Jesus.
In silence the candles are lit.
Let us pray:
We worship you, Lord, we praise your holy name.
In the gift of your Son Jesus
you have shown us your everlasting love for us.
As a father cares for his child, as a mother cradles her offspring, so
you tenderly reach out to each one of us with the arms of love.
When we reject your love and turn away from you,
gently you call us back, rejoicing when we accept your love.
With every generation, past, present and future,
we worship you, Lord, and praise your holy name.   **Amen**

Offering Prayer

Lord we bring these gifts from our wealth of blessings.
    Accept and use them to feed the hungry,
    and to give good things to the poor,
    the discouraged and the unloved
    in this community and across the world.   **Amen**

Prayers of Thanksgiving

Lord, you have done so much for us and we give you our thanks.
We thank you for your care of all your faithful people,
who through many generations have rejoiced in your love.

We thank you for turning upside down the ways of the world.
You provide for the poor and hungry,
  give strength to the weak,
  humble the arrogant,
  and bring good in place of evil.

We thank you for the unexpected ways you reveal yourself.
You promised to come and your promise was fulfilled,
  you came as a baby born of a woman,
  died in misery on a cross,
  and opened the door of heaven in the resurrection.

We thank you for the ways you care for us.
You have saved us from our sin,
  filled us with your Spirit,
  listened to our prayers,
  and given us the blessing of eternal life.

You raise us from sadness to joy,
  so that we can laugh at our enemies,
  and hold our heads high as your friends.
Thank you, Lord, for your mighty acts of love.   **Amen**

'Who am I?'   (*Luke 1.43*)

Who am I, Mighty God, that you should come to me?
I am no one special,
I am no one important,
and yet you came into the world for me.
I am filled with your blessings,
saved by your mercy and given life by your love.
Thank you for making me in your image
and caring for me as your child.   **Amen**

Blessing

Grace and peace to you from God our Father
and the Lord Jesus Christ.   **Amen**

Christmas Day

Presentation

Place the star either by a crib scene or on the cross. The positioning of a crib scene beside a cross will help to link the incarnation to the gift of salvation offered by Jesus.

Call to Worship   (*Luke 2.10, 11, 14*)

I bring you good news, news of great joy for the whole nation. Today there has been born to you in the city of David a deliverer – the Messiah, the Lord. Glory to God in the highest heaven, and on earth peace to all in whom God delights.

Advent Candle Prayer   *Read by those who light the candles.*
Light the first four candles.

The great day has arrived!
The long wait for the Lord's coming is over. During the past weeks we have heard how the Jews waited, how the Bible revealed the Messiah, how John the Baptist prepared the way, how Mary rejoiced to know she would give birth to God's Son. Now we light this final candle to celebrate the birth of Jesus, the Son of God, born of a woman, a child and yet a king who comes to claim his kingdom.
In silence the fifth candle is lit.

Let us pray; after each phrase the response is:	**Praise God**
For the gift of his Son;	**Praise God**
He who was promised long ago has come;	**Praise God**
He brings justice and peace;	**Praise God**
In him is the Word made flesh;	**Praise God**
He is the Light of the world;	**Praise God**
For in him we see our Father;	**Praise God**
In him our sins are forgiven;	**Praise God**
Through him we shall be saved;	**Praise God**
With all the angels we shout for joy;	**Praise God**
We praise your name today and for evermore;	**Praise God**

Prayer of Wonder at the Manger   *Use different voices.*

Mary gave birth to a Son and wrapped him in swaddling cloths. We marvel, Loving God, that you came as a tiny baby!

How could you, the mighty God, come in such a humble form?
You came to be like us, to know our joys and sorrows!

The angels praised God and announced peace on earth.
We rejoice, Loving God, that through the child, born in Bethlehem
and laid in a manger, you brought peace to a suffering world,
a mysterious peace which transformed history and changes our
lives.

The shepherds ran to see for themselves what had happened.
We thank you, Loving God, for the good news of a Saviour
welcomed with joy by the shepherds, proved in our own experience
and intended for the deliverance of all humankind.

We gather here to worship at the manger.
We wonder, Loving Lord, at the mystery of your presence in Jesus
and at the love you have revealed
through his life and teaching, his death and resurrection.
As we treasure all these things and ponder them,
help us to learn, to grow and to live
in the knowledge that you are with us.   **Amen**

Meditation on the Word

Many words are spoken at Christmas:
words of greeting, words of love,
words telling the story of Jesus.
And words are powerful –
   to express love or hate,
   to inspire or depress,
   to build up or destroy,
   to join us to God in prayer.
Jesus was the Word made flesh.
The Word who created the universe,
   who brought light and life to all,
   who told us of God and the Father's love,
   who speaks for us at God's right hand.
May our words never obscure the word which God has spoken in
Christ.

Closing Prayer

You are the children of God,
made sons and daughters through the Sonship of Christ.
Go and share your Christmas joy with a world longing to hear good
news. In the name of God, Father, Son and Holy Spirit.   **Amen**

1st Sunday after Christmas

Presentation

Use a wide variety of Christmas card and other pictures to help the congregation to explore and share their thoughts of what the visit of the Magi to Bethlehem might have been like.

Call to Worship   *(Isa. 49.13)*

'Shout for joy, you heavens; earth rejoice;
break into songs of triumph, you mountains,
for the Lord has comforted his people.'
Let us join with the whole creation to praise God.

Prayer of Adoration

Wonder of wonders, mighty God, that you should come to this world!
Holy, pure, just – your feet walked it, your hands touched it.
The very idea! Our minds cannot grasp it; we need your help.
So fill us with your Spirit that we are set free to wonder, and adore you.
Wonder of wonders, mighty God, that you should come as you did!
The creator of all – to share our flesh and blood!
We need your Spirit's help to see it, and take it in …
Born, just like every one of us, yet how much more;
born to draw love from loving hearts,
born to draw worship from trusting and adoring hearts,
born to draw fear and hatred, too, from hardened hearts;
born to bring love to those who know they need it,
born to bring judgment to those who cling fast to the world and reject your love;
born in time, to be the Lord, the Saviour, the Judge of us all;
born to be the Way, the Truth and the Life for us all.
God of wonders, our minds cannot grasp, our words struggle
and fail …
We need your help. Set our spirits free by your Spirit
to see, to wonder, to adore.   **Amen**

Prayer of Praise and Thanksgiving

Father God, we thank you for the way in which the Magi came to
Bethlehem:
- for their constant searching for the truth;
- for their openness to the new vision you gave them in the star;
- for their persistence in searching, even though the journey was
  hard;
- for their faith persuading them to open their treasures, in such an
  unlikely place.

We thank you for revealing Jesus to strangers from other lands, and
showing us that he is Lord and Saviour of all the nations.   **Amen**

Prayer of Intercession and Petition

Listening God, we pray for people today who are travelling as
pilgrims through this world, searching for truth and faith:
- encourage them when others discourage;
- enable them to persist in the hard parts of their journey;
- give them faith to follow their way when it leads in unlikely
  directions;
- reveal yourself in your own way to all who truly search for you.

Loving God, help us to love you and worship you with open minds.
Save us from thinking we know it all. Help us to be ready to catch
your vision for our lives, our church, our community, and to travel
in faith as you lead us. Remind us that the end of all our travelling
is to be with you in unlimited fellowship, to see you as you are, to
enjoy your light and love for ever. Bless us in our pilgrimage; keep
us travelling in faith.   **Amen**

Offering Prayer

Gracious God, our money seems so ordinary compared with gold,
frankincense and myrrh. Yet it is what we have, and we give it in
humility and worship. Use our ordinary gifts in the extraordinary
service of your kingdom.   **Amen**

Dismissal

Go your way; travel in faith; walk in the light of God.

2nd Sunday after Christmas

Presentation

Imagine yourself the editor of a newspaper which reports only good news. Invite the congregation to offer their contributions, writing them up on a flipchart or overhead projector. Make this a brainstorm of praise.

Call to Worship   (*I Thess. 2.4*)

'God has approved us as fit to be entrusted with the gospel.'
We praise God for his trust and listen for the Good News he has for us.

Prayer of Confession

Forgiving God, you have entrusted us with such Good News. The Bible contains your word to us: you have inspired people to write, copy, translate, publish and distribute its books. You have called men and women to study, write and speak to bring the gospel to us. So often we have thanked you in words for the Good News, and stopped there.

So often we have taken the Good News of your life-changing love for granted. It has become ordinary to us and we have forgotten how amazing it is. We have not been thrilled by it, and so we have kept it to ourselves.

So often we have allowed ourselves to be discouraged from sharing the gospel: we have given up in the face of opposition, indifference and difficulties.

Forgive us for our dullness, our lack of joy and sparkle.
Help us to stop – now – to recall the Good News you give us.
Pause
Help us to hear it again with open ears;
Help us to let your Spirit in to sparkle within us and bring us new life.   **Amen**

Prayer of Praise and Thanksgiving

Loving God, we thank you for your deep love for us, accepting each of us, with no one too young or too old for your loving care. We thank you for growth and maturing. Sometimes growing up or growing older is painful for us, but we thank you that at different stages of our lives you enable us to see and understand things in ways that change and develop. We thank you that our different experiences give us different things to share with others older and younger than ourselves, and that in this sharing we can help one another and enrich one another's lives. We thank you for our families and the helpfulness you intend between the generations; for the times we have specially enjoyed being together and doing things together.

We thank you for times in our church when we have taken the trouble to arrange events for younger and older people together; when we have learned about one another and from one another; when we have enjoyed being together in your family.

Remind us of your intention for us; that we should each be a part of your one family all the days of our lives.   **Amen**

Prayer of Intercession

God, parent of all, we pray for those who are parents.

We pray for parents who carry the responsibilities of bringing up children alone.
L: In the bright times and the dark: R: **God, be there for them.**

We pray for parents wanting to do all that they should for very young children, yet wondering whether they are succeeding.
L: In the bright times and the dark: R: **God, be there for them.**

We pray for parents delighting that the potential of growing and teenage children is being fulfilled, yet anxious about the temptations they face.
L: In the bright times and the dark: R: **God, be there for them.**

We pray for parents sharing the delight and pain of children who have started their own families, yet needing to keep a difficult distance.
L: In the bright times and the dark: R: **God, be there for them.**

We pray for all parents, that they may always be open to learn from their children, and from their own special experiences.
L: In the bright times and the dark: R: **God, be there for them.**

Dismissal

It has been good for us to be in our Father's house.
Go out now, to love and serve him.

1st Sunday after Epiphany

Presentation

Present a mime of a rescue at sea in which a person is saved from drowning and lifted safely from the water to begin life again.

Call to Worship   (*I John 5.6*)

'Jesus Christ is the one who came with the water of his baptism and the blood of his death.'
Let us thank God for the wonder and mystery of the gift of his Son.

Prayer of Adoration

Mighty, saving God, you work great wonders to rescue your people.
We rejoice because of what you have done in our lives. When we have been in difficulties and have brought our concerns to you, you have rescued us and brought us safely through them. You have done for us more than we could ever imagine or hope for. You have never let us down. *Pause*
When we see you at work in our lives we are amazed. Yet you have shown us in the Bible that you have always rescued and saved your people in their times of need. We rejoice because of the great things you have done. You rescued your people long ago from their slavery in Egypt.
Your love, your compassion and your power combined to set them free and lead them on their journey with Moses, the leader you had given them.
You saved them from the Egyptian army, leading them safely through the sea.
You gave them water to drink and food to eat in the desert.
You drew them together as your people and gave them your laws to govern their lives.
You kept your promise and led them through Jordan to their own land.
Mighty, saving, faithful God, we adore you. *Pause*
You have given us Jesus to be our Saviour, the rescuer of people of every land and race to put their trust in him.
He rescues us from ignorance by revealing what you are like.

He rescues us from fear by rising triumphant over death.
He rescues us from our sins by meeting repentance with
forgiveness.
He rescues us from loneliness by offering his constant friendship.
Mighty, saving, faithful God, give us your Spirit to open our eyes,
for you are wonderful beyond our imagining and we come to
worship and adore you.   **Amen**

Prayer of Praise and Thanksgiving

God, Father of Jesus and our Father,
L: We give you our thanks: R: **Your love is eternal.**
For your Spirit moving in Jesus as he grew, leading him to become
more aware of you, his Father,
L: We give you our thanks: R: **Your love is eternal.**
For Jesus coming to the Jordan to be baptized by John; for his
humility in being baptized with people repenting of their sins; for
your Spirit coming upon Jesus like a dove and for the voice from
heaven, so that we know who Jesus is,
L: We give you our thanks: R: **Your love is eternal.**
For accepting infants, young people, adults into the family of your
church through the sacrament of baptism,
L: We give you our thanks: R: **Your love is eternal.**
For recuing us from darkness and death into your light and eternal
life through the waters of baptism,
L: We give you our thanks: R: **Your love is eternal.**

Offering prayer

Generous God, Jesus gave his life to you in his baptism, and
surrendered himself to the driving of your Spirit. Let the Spirit
drive us, too, as we live and give for you.   **Amen**

Dismissal

The Spirit drove Jesus out into the desert to be tested.
Go now, in the Spirit's power, to meet the world's testing.

2nd Sunday after Epiphany

Presentation

Today's readings are about people being arrested by God. Try an interview with someone – preferably a member of a local Christian congregation – with a story to tell about how God arrested them.

Call to Worship   (*Mark 1.15*)

'The right time has come, and the kingdom of God is near!
Turn away from your sins and believe the Good News!'

Prayer of Confession

Forgiving God, sometimes when your Spirit has stirred us, and called us to do something to serve you, we have recognized it and said, 'Yes'. Then we have known the joy and peace within us that come from doing something for you. Maybe it was just a little thing to share your love in a practical way with someone else, but we have done it and been glad.

Other times when you have tugged at us and shown us something you need doing we have said, 'Not me … I can't', because we were frightened by it. It seemed so big, so far beyond anything we ever thought we could do.

Perhaps it was to help someone with real problems we felt we couldn't handle …

Or to lead, or speak to, groups of people and we felt afraid to face them …

Perhaps it was a part in the ministry of the church and we worried about what other people might think …

Or something demanding a lot of our time and we were afraid we would have no time left for our families or ourselves …

Perhaps it was something needing study and new skills and we were afraid we would fail …

Or something else that we recall now in quietness … *Pause*

Forgive us for our fear; forgive us when we have closed our hands and our hearts against your call. Help us to trust you to know best about what we can do and become for you … *Pause*

Thank you for the good news that you forgive everyone who
sincerely asks.
Thank you for forgiving us.   **Amen**

Prayer of Petition

God, the giver of all good gifts, help us to recognize your gifts ...
gifts for helping; gifts for teaching; gifts for speaking; gifts for
healing; gifts for administration; gifts for sharing your love; gifts
for encouraging and bringing out the best in others.
Draw us closer together in our fellowship so that we can help each
other to recognize and use the gifts you have given each of us.
Then help us to adventure in living, giving, and serving you,
trusting that you will not let us down or forsake us.   **Amen**

Meditation

What do you want *me* to do for you, Lord?
I really want to serve you, and do something for you ... But what?
Jeremiah became a prophet – he had the gifts all right, despite his
fear. He carried on, even when it hurt.
Paul became an apostle, a church planter, a theologian. You
arrested him and turned him round. The results are plain to see!
Simon, Andrew, James and John became disciples, apostles, leaders
of the church. For all their mistakes, and times you had to correct
them, they were mighty for you!
But me? What can I do for you, Lord?
Listen, my child; it's not really like that.
Those others, they put themselves in my hands;
I gave them the gifts and I did the rest.
Just stay close to me; listen to me in scripture,
in your prayers, speaking through your Christian friends,
calling through the world and its needs and hurts.
Risk yourself in my hands; trust me.
Then you'll serve me as I want you to; serve me as I know you can.

Dismissal

Jesus called his first disciples to follow him.
He is calling you, too. Follow him and trust him.

3rd Sunday after Epiphany

Presentation

*Ask a group to present a brief drama. A family with a problem talks,
worries, argues, and prays about it. Eventually a solution emerges.
In his own time and way God has answered their prayers.*

Call to Worship   (*I Peter 1.3*)

'Let us give thanks to the God and Father of our Lord Jesus Christ!
Because of his great mercy he gave us new life by raising Jesus
Christ from death.'

Prayer of Praise and Thanksgiving

God of light, we thank you and praise you because you have not
hidden yourself from us. We do not have to guess or grope in
darkness, or turn to superstition and magic to try to find you. You
have plainly told us and shown us what you are like and what you
ask of us.
We praise and thank you for the laws you have given us to rule our
lives and relationships. We do not have to search high and low for
them; they are there in scripture for us to read and hear.
We praise and thank you for Jesus, your living word, and for all
that we see of your love and power in his death and resurrection,
and for the new life and eternal blessings you give to us in him.
We praise and thank you for inspiring people like Peter and Paul to
write, helping us to understand more about what you have done for
us in Jesus, and what you ask of us.
Help us to show our thanks by choosing your way of light and
life.   **Amen**

Prayer of Confession

Patient God, we know in our hearts and minds that you have told
us how you want us to live. Your commands are part of your
loving plan for us, and are meant to be obeyed.
But we have not always obeyed you.
Sometimes we have been deliberately selfish and flouted your
commands because they were inconvenient and got in our way.

L: God, be patient with us:
R: **Forgive us and help us in your love**.
Sometimes we have forgotten your teaching in the heat of an argument, and have lashed out blindly at someone else, wanting to hurt them.
L: God, be patient with us:
R: **Forgive us and help us in your love**.
Sometimes we have seen things happening that we knew were against your commands, and have kept quiet because we were afraid.
L: God, be patient with us:
R: **Forgive us and help us in your love**.
Sometimes when we have known about events in the world we have not thought of testing them against the standard of your laws.
L: God, be patient with us:
R: **Forgive us and help us in your love**.
Help us to be honest with you about the times we have let you down, so that we may receive your forgiveness and make a fresh start.
L: God, be patient with us:
R: **Forgive us and help us in your love**.

Prayer of Intercession

Listening God, we pray for those who continue Christ's work of teaching about your kingdom. Enable them to overcome problems and grasp opportunities. Help them to be true to the gospel message. May their words be like seeds taking root in good ground, yielding rich harvests of Christian disciples.
We pray especially for those who teach new converts and people who have never had the opportunity of taking Jesus seriously. May their words come with your authority, to lead young and old alike out of the ways of evil and death into your ways of goodness and life.   **Amen**

Dismissal

Choose life,
love the Lord your God;
obey him
and hold fast to him.   **Amen**

4th Sunday after Epiphany

Presentation

*Encourage the congregation to share with you and each other
instances of different kinds of giving to their church – for instance,
gifts of costly furnishings, large and small contributions of money,
offerings of regular, dedicated, service.*

Call to Worship   (*I Chron. 29.11*)

'Yours, Lord, is the greatness and the power,
the glory, the splendour and the majesty;
for everything in heaven and on earth is yours;
yours, Lord, is the sovereignty and you are exalted over all as
head.'
This is our God, and we worship him now.

Prayer of Adoration

Wonderful God, sometimes when we come to church we forget
why we have come. We enjoy meeting and talking with other
people, and that has its place. We want to talk about matters in the
life and work of our church, and that, too, is necessary.
But the reason we really come together is to worship you.
Help us now as we stop to take that in. *Pause*
Help us as we try to put everything else out of our minds. *Pause*
Help us as we worship and adore you. *Pause*
You are great ... you are powerful ... you are the King of kings ...
you rule over all as the head of all ... you know everything ...
you know us ... and yet you love us ... you are with us wherever
we go.
Wonderful God, we cannot understand you, but we love you, we
worship and adore you.   **Amen**

Prayer of Confession

Loving God, our bodies are 'temples of the Holy Spirit'. They are
as important as that!
Help us as we stop to think about what that means. *Pause*
We know that we do not always respect our own bodies enough,

and we live in a world where people abuse their own bodies and those of others.

We do not keep our bodies properly nourished and exercised; we consume too much junk food and ignore the effect on our bodies.

We do not know or care enough about additives and their effect on our food.

Some people over-eat and damage their bodies; others undermine their health by following unwise diets.

Some are deprived of sufficient wholesome food altogether by poverty; others become slaves of drugs and ruin their bodies.

We confess, to you the wrong doing and wrong thinking of your human family.

Forgive us, help us to see your way and follow it.   **Amen**

Prayer of Intercession

Healing God, we offer you our prayers for all who are working for the healing of your children:
– those who have dedicated themselves to combatting diseases;
– researchers involved in discovering and developing new
   treatments;
– all kinds of staff working long hours in hospitals;
– doctors, nurses, physiotherapists, administrators and others
   working in local medical practices;
– psychiatrists and others committed to healing mental illnesses;
– those working with people to heal the scars left by memories and
   hurts deep within.

All true healing work is part of your loving purpose, and we ask your blessing and help for all who are involved in it.   **Amen**

Offering Prayer

Eternal God, your people in times past gave willingly and generously.

Accept and bless our giving when it is willing and generous.   **Amen**

Dismissal   *(I Cor. 6.19,20)*

'You do not belong to yourselves, but to God; he bought you for a price.'

Go now; let your living be to his glory.

5th Sunday after Epiphany

II Sam. 12.1–13
I Peter 1.22–25
Mark 4.10–12, 21–34

Presentation

*Nathan's confrontation with David in today's Old Testament
passage cries out for dramatized reading. You will need three
readers (Narrator, Nathan, David). Encourage them to bring out all
the changing moods from the narrative.*

Call to Worship   (*I Peter 1.23*)

'Through the living and eternal word of God you have been born
again as children of a parent who is immortal.'
We praise God for his word and his love.

Prayer of Praise and Thanksgiving

Gracious God, we praise you because you are not silent. You do
not hide from us, or leave us without your message. You have
called and appointed men and women to be your prophets, to speak
out for you to the people of their own time.
L: For your prophets in our time:
R: **We praise you and thank you**.
You have given your prophets your own messages to declare.
L: For your prophets in our time:
R: **We praise you and thank you**.
You have given them boldness and courage to bring difficult and
unpopular messages.
L: For your prophets in our time:
R: **We praise you and thank you**.
You have stood with them, when without you they would have
turned away from their task.
L: For your prophets in our time:
R: **We praise you and thank you**.
Thank you for all those who speak to us in your name.   **Amen**

Prayer of Confession

Merciful God, you have set your truth before us in many different
ways:
– through the words of the Bible;

- through the words of preachers, teachers and leaders in the church;
- through the voice of your Holy Spirit speaking within us;
- through the voices of family, friends and other people we meet;
- through the events of the world reported in the news media.

We realize that we need to confess to you that so often we are deaf to what you say to us, because we are not expecting you to speak, or because we deliberately choose not to hear.
Forgive us, and help us to keep alert, expecting to hear you speak. Help us to take notice of what you say, even if it is uncomfortable and hard to hear. Help us to see the truth you speak to us in your love.   **Amen**

Prayer of Intercession

Loving God, we offer you our prayers for those who are your messengers today. Bless them – give to them your own resources of courage, truth, and love. May they look at the world with clear eyes and listen for your prompting with open ears.
May they see your truth and speak out boldly in your name:
- in the church when we are going astray and failing you;
- in the community when people are hurting others and being hurt;
- in the nation when we are turning from your ways of love and peace;
- in the world when people are being oppressed and denied justice.

Continue to call men and women to be your messengers.
Help us to hear and obey your message coming through their words.   **Amen**

Offering Prayer

Generous God, in your giving to us you have far exceeded anything we could ever think of giving to you. May each of us let what we give to you be inspired by what you give to us.   **Amen**

Dismissal

Love one another;
dwell in Christ;
let Christ dwell in you.

6th Sunday after Epiphany

Presentation

Religious practices are meaningless without active commitment to doing God's will. Illustrate through discussion with congregation, or demonstration, that in making bread following the precise details of the recipe is useless without yeast, the active ingredient.

Call to Worship (*John 4.24*)

'God is Spirit, and those who worship him must worship in spirit and in truth.'
Let us offer him our worship.

Prayer of Adoration

Holy God, you are faithful and true.
You are not one thing today and another tomorrow; you do not pretend to be one thing whilst being another.
You are just and fair. You are against those who treat others cruelly or unfairly; you are on the side of those who are refused justice and denied the basic rights of human beings.
You see clearly right into the heart of everything. You see clearly into our lives and minds. When we hurt others, you know; when we ourselves are hurt, you know that, too.
Yet even though you know each of us and everything about us, you still go on loving us and wanting us to become more like you. That is the utter wonder of your gracious love.
As we come to see more about you, we want to love you more, and adore you more for your justice, fairness and love. As we want to grow more like you, give us the Holy Spirit to help us.   **Amen**

Prayer of Intercession

Father God, we pray today for all victims of injustice, poverty and neglect.
We pray for unwanted children and for the parents who do not love them:
> for children terrified by their parents' quarrels and arguments;
> for children abused and in danger of permanent injury or death;
> for street children living in constant fear of injury or murder.

L: Help them, Father: R: **They are our brothers and sisters**.

We pray for all those suffering unfair treatment and discrimination:
> because of their accent, their clothes, their customs and practices,
> their home address, the colour of their skin, and their lack
> of people skilled to represent and support them.

L: Help them, Father: R: **They are our brothers and sisters**.

We pray for those who, through famine and drought, face starvation:
who, without supplies of clean water, are at risk of disease;
who lack opportunities of education or proper health care;
who are poorly paid to grow export crops which make others rich.

L: Help them, Father: R: **They are our brothers and sisters**.

When we worship you, help us to set our minds on pleasing you, not ourselves. Help us to 'hunger and thirst to see right prevail'.   **Amen**

Offering Prayer

Holy God, empty words and empty gestures do not please you.
So bless us that we may give ourselves as well as our money in the cause of truth, integrity, and justice.   **Amen**

Dismissal

Go; follow the Spirit's leading as you make life's choices.

9th Sunday before Easter

Presentation

Prepare two or three people from different age groups to speak briefly about the wisdom they have gained from experiences at particular times. Conclude how much greater is God's wisdom than the sum of ours.

Call to Worship   (*I Cor. 2.9*)

'What no one ever saw or heard, what no one ever thought could happen, is the very thing God prepared for those who love him.' We show our love for him as we worship him now.

Prayer of Adoration

Living God, in wonder we adore you.
Before you made the universe in all its vastness, you had a plan, a purpose. It did not all just happen: you imagined it, designed it.
L: Living God: R: **We marvel at your wisdom.**   *Pause*
You created the universe in all its tiny details, too. Whether we look up to the stars or down to the tiniest plant, we see your work of planning and design.
L: Living God: R: **We marvel at your wisdom.**   *Pause*
You created living creatures – birds, fish, animals, insects, human beings – a splendour of variety. You created each of us. When we think of how our bodies work, our brains function, we are amazed. You are the designer and maker of it all.
L: Living God: R: **We marvel at your wisdom.**   *Pause*
You show yourself to us, telling us through Jesus that you are our loving Father, and leading us to be your children and your friends.
L: Living God: R: **We marvel at your wisdom.**   *Pause*   **Amen**

Prayer of Petition

Loving God, providing for all our needs, help us not just to admire your wisdom or marvel at it. Give to us your Holy Spirit, the Spirit of truth:
– to lead us into your truth;
– to help us to want to know more of your wisdom;
– to help us to take seriously all the ways you show us your

wisdom;
– to lead us to accept the authority of Jesus, teaching us your truth;
– to prompt us to read, listen carefully, and take in the words of
Jesus;
– to guide us in obeying and carrying out his teaching in our own
lives.
When we ask for your Holy Spirit, may we be ready to let him in to
work in us.   **Amen**

Meditation

'Immortal, invisible, God only wise'

How grand that sounds, Lord! Yet a bit off-putting somehow.
It makes you sound so far away, so far above me.
You must be clever – very clever indeed – to have done all you
have ... conceived, planned, designed and made – literally
everything.
And you are still involved in its continuing creation, its evolution,
and you sustain it all from day to day.
I know you are very clever; and yet I find some clever people a
little frightening, not easy to feel comfortable with.
Your clever wisdom makes me feel like that sometimes.
      There is a difference you need to know, my child, between being
clever and being wise.
Cleverness can be cold, remote; while wisdom is warm and close at
hand.
That's what I want you to know and trust that I am – warm, loving,
close at hand, there for you.
My wisdom is part of my love – for you and everything I've made.
Mine is the wisdom of long experience, that says, 'I know, for I've
been there'.
Mine is the wisdom of knowing what's best for you;
mine the love that wants you to know it, too.

Dismissal

Go in peace;
open your ears, listen to Jesus.

8th Sunday before Easter

Presentation

Cut large pictures from newspaper and magazine advertisements for cosmetics, medicines, hair and body and dental care preparations. Use them to pose the question, 'What do you mean by health and wholeness?'

Call to Worship   *Based on Ps. 147.1*

Praise the Lord!
How good it is to sing the praises of our God!
How right and joyful it is to praise him!

Prayer of Praise and Thanksgiving

God, great in power, overflowing with love and compassion, we praise you, we thank you, for your wonders of healing. We thank you especially for the healing work of Jesus:
– that he showed us how you want all your children to be well;
– that he healed illnesses affecting people's bodies;
– that he showed us how illnesses which affect our bodies can be linked to deeper causes in our minds and spirits;
– that he healed people whose minds were ill;
– that he healed those affected by evil spirits;
– that he brought inner healing to those not at peace with you, others, or themselves.
We praise you because you have entrusted the healing work of Jesus to his followers in the church. We thank you that you still want your children to be whole. We praise you for everything that is done today in the name of Jesus to bring healing to bodies, minds, and spirits.   **Amen**

Prayer of Confession

Loving God, we need your help to see those things in our lives, especially those deep within us, that need your healing.
We offer ourselves to you now in quietness.   *Pause*

We offer to you our broken relationships with other people – all the
hurts and resentments, all the painful memories, that may go back
over many years; all the anger, like strong acid eating us away
inside.   *Pause*
We offer to you our broken relationship with ourselves – the times
when we don't like ourselves, and find it hard to believe that other
people can really love us, or that you can love us either.   *Pause*
We offer to you our broken relationship with you – the times when
we have disappointed you and let you down; when we have not
prayed to you or trusted you; when we have deliberately turned our
backs on you.   *Pause*
We ask for the Holy Spirit to come and work deep within us:
– to help us to see our need to forgive and our need to ask for
   forgiveness;
– to reach deep within us to heal the hurts, the memories, the
   anger;
– and to enfold us in your healing love.   **Amen**

Prayer of Petition

Healing God, we ask you to give us greater faith and trust in your
power to heal. Help us to see how our church can be a community
of people working with you to bring help and healing to others:
– to people who are hurting and afraid;
– to people who are lonely;
– to people who are searching for you.
Help us to see where our church needs healing:
– when people do not feel welcome or comfortable with us;
– when we quarrel and hurt each other;
– when we hold back your work in our neighbourhood by our
   selfishness and lack of faith.
Help us to trust that you do want your people to be healed and
whole. Help us to trust that you do have the power to heal us, and
all your people – if we will let you.   **Amen**

Dismissal

Go on praying for one another,
so that you will be healed
in body, mind and spirit.

7th Sunday before Easter

Presentation

Using a flip-chart or overhead projector draw a TV-type weather map complete with symbols. Use the symbols as metaphors for our varied experiences of life.

Call to Worship   *(Ps. 95.1.2)*

'Come, let us praise the Lord! Let us sing for joy to God who protects us!
Let us come before him with thankfulness, and sing joyful songs of praise!'

Prayer of Adoration

Awesome God of power, you are the Lord of winds and waves and all the forces of nature. You created the earth, with its skies, seas and dry land, full of energy and movement.
The rushing wind, the pouring rain, the flashing lightning, the rumbling thunder, the pounding sea, the surging river currents ... you made them all.
Sometimes they frighten, sometimes fascinate and delight us. We cannot always control, yet often use their tremendous power. But as we worship and adore you, maker of all, show us your love as well as your power.   **Amen**

Prayer of Confession   *(After the reading from Jonah)*

Forgiving, patient God, you speak to us through the words of the Bible, yet time and again we do not take in what you are saying to us. We read the story of Jonah, but we do not learn from his mistakes.
He thought he could get away from you by taking a ship. He thought there were places where you couldn't reach him with your command to do what he didn't want to do. We sometimes think we can escape from you, ignore you, or get away with living our lives our own way all the time. Help us to learn from Jonah's story that

you are everywhere; there before us to turn us back wherever we
try to run.

Jonah thought you couldn't possibly love his enemies. He wanted
to stop you wasting your love on them! Yet when he went to
Nineveh he was amazed that the people listened to him. Sometimes
we think we know better than you about whom you love. We think
that because we don't like some people or the way they live that
you don't love them. Help us to learn from Jonah's story that you
love even the most unlikable people.

Forgive us; be patient with us; help us to learn from you.   **Amen**

Prayer of Intercession

Listening God, hear our prayers for people facing storms in life
today. We pray for those whose work takes them into danger from
storms of weather: crews of ships, oil rigs, aeroplanes; workers in
rescue services – lifeboats, helicopters, mountain rescue teams.

L: Listening God, hear our prayer: R: **Come and listen to us.***

We pray for those working with others in storms of conflict:
carrying out delicate negotiations between hostile nations or
groups;

working to bring peace between workers and employers;
caught up in painful conflict in the church.

L: Listening God, hear our prayer: R: **Come and listen to us.***

We pray for those facing storms in their personal and family lives:
people who are worried and anxious, distressed and afraid;
people living in difficult neighbourhoods;
people whose marriage and family relationships are difficult.

L: Listening God, hear our prayer: R: **Come and listen to us.***
Amen

Offering Prayer

Creator God, you are Lord of all. You have no need of us, yet you
choose to accept and use everything we offer in our love for you.
Accept the offering of our lives and money for your work of love
today.   **Amen**

Dismissal

Hold on firmly to the truths you have heard,
so that you will not drift from your course.

---

* Or use Taizé chant 'O Lord, hear my prayer'.

6th Sunday before Easter
Lent 1

Presentation

*Posters from aid agencies, slides with appropriate music, or mime,
could be used to emphasize the contrast of pulling down and
uprooting/ building and planting – possibly in prayers.*

Prayer of Confession

God of justice and compassion,
you have set your law within us,
written it in our hearts, not only in tablets of stone;
yet we still break faith with your covenant of care,
acting unjustly, forgetting
that our neighbours will know your love
not through our teaching, but through our living.
We have failed you. Forgive us.   *Silence*

Living God,
We remember your love shown in the life of Jesus,
as he shared the test of our suffering, as he died for our sins.
We remember that your justice
is always tempered with compassion.
We remember your promise
that you will forgive your people's wrongdoing
and our sins you will call to mind no more.
And we thank you.

Prayer of Adoration

God of infinite power;
you created the universe, and our planet spinning within it,
the world, and men and women walking upon it.
Your energy knows no bounds – it is beyond our imagination,
creative, amazing, even terrifying.
You have the power to pull down and uproot,
to demolish and destroy and inflict disaster.

Yet we find you, time and again, watching over your creation,
willing it to survive, waiting to build and to plant –
to break the power of death and to bring hope:
God of infinite hope.   **Amen**

Prayer of Praise and Thanksgiving

Creator God,
through you all things have their being;
for you earth and sky, flowing water and green growing things
and every living creature exist,
so that, by their very being, they may praise you.
So, with all creation, in all our lives, we praise you.

Jesus our Saviour,
you came to share our lives,
crossed the bridge from Creator to creation,
took on flesh and blood
and called us your sisters and brothers;
for us you broke the power of death and set us free
to become whole in our humanity and to live in your way,
and, when we do so, we praise you.

Holy Spirit,
moving where Christians gather,
liberating and encouraging,
changing and consecrating,
may we fulfil God's promise in us
richly, creatively
and, even so, praise you.   **Amen**

Dismissal

Send us out, Lord,
with your law written on our hearts,
send us out to live your gospel.   **Amen**

5th Sunday before Easter
Lent 2

Presentation

*All ages could enjoy a visual demonstration of the 'armour of God'
– donning belt, shield, helmet etc. (or modern equivalents), or using
flipchart or felt-board – but do not neglect the qualities they
represent!*

Call to Worship

Find your strength in the Lord ...
stand fast ... and pray always in the power of the Spirit.   **Amen**

Prayer of Adoration and Confession

Great God, you have set us in a world full of wonder,
but we walk through it with closed minds and hearts.
You give us a fertile earth, where we could lead fruitful lives,
but we waste the opportunities, pollute water and air.
You offer us order, and we return to chaos.
You surround us with glory, and we worship worthless gods.
You are a source of living water, and we put our faith
in cracked cisterns where nothing of value is safe.
Forgive us.
Through Jesus, the Way, the Life, Light and Living Water,
We believe we are forgiven: **Thanks be to God**.

Meditation

There isn't much call for armour now,
as there was when a knight won his spurs.
Suits of armour are picturesque –
we have other ways of hurting each other,
and much of the time we live in a kind of guarded peace.
But there is still conflict, in our world and in our hearts,
still the need to live in God's way, in God's strength.
So let me take truth, to be at the centre
and to hold together all I try to do.

Let me take integrity, to protect me
from my own false moves, and to be a sign
of your Way that I'm not ashamed to wear.
Let me put on the shoes of the gospel of peace,
not just to walk quietly and steadily with you as my guide,
but maybe to walk a mile in the shoes of someone else.
Let me take faith, much more than a piece of military hardwear,
as needful and everyday as soap and water or a roof over my head.
Let me take salvation in my heart as well as on my head.
And let me take the one weapon God gives, the Word,
a two-edged sword which pierces the pretence of my own life,
while it goes straight to the heart of the matter, for everyone.
Living Word, grant me the right words when I speak,
and your strong presence in the symbols of everyday.   **Amen**

Prayer of Intercession

Loving God, as your church we are committed
to keep watch and intercede for the world.

We pray now for politicians, church leaders and all
in positions of power that they may act responsibly,
seeking only the welfare of others and the glory of your holy name.

We pray for the powerless – for the poor, the lonely,
the disabled, the homeless (etc.) – that they may find
justice and peace, know your love and be strengthened
to glorify your name.

And we pray for ourselves, in our strength and in our weakness,
that we may be neither complacent nor despairing
but may recognize your presence in every part of our lives
so that all we do, for ourselves and for others,
may be to the glory of your name.   **Amen**

Dismissal

Jesus said 'Whoever does the will of God is my brother and sister
and mother.'
God has called us his family: go, to do God's will in the world.

4th Sunday before Easter
Lent 3

Presentation

A creed/affirmation of faith could be a central part of service; maybe take a fresh look at it, phrase by phrase. If chapel has an appropriate text painted on the wall, or embroidered on a banner, use that as focus.

Prayer of Adoration   (*Could be linked to Hymns and Psalms 257*)

God, our Creator, source of our life,
    you are a rock, a shield,
    a safe protecting place;
    your love is hidden treasure, infinite riches.
Jesus, Lord of life,
    you are prophet and priest,
    connecting heaven and earth,
    but also our brother, our friend,
    our gentle shepherd,
    feeding us when we are hungry,
    healing us when we are hurt.
Holy Spirit, Breath of life,
    you encourage us, with all God's people,
    to travel in the way,
    to dance to the music,
    and to praise our Maker.
May we, while we have breath,
    respond to your love,
    receive your encouragement
    and rejoice in the good news of your salvation.   **Amen**

Prayer of Confession

Strong and sheltering God, bearing up our lives,
    on you we can lean for support.
    We call ourselves your people
    but often are ashamed to name you.

Just and merciful God, source of judgment and forgiveness,
  to you we can turn in our weakness.
  We call ourselves citizens of your kingdom
  but often are ashamed to name you.
Living and beckoning God, changer of our lives,
  your challenging questions prompt our faith.
  We can call you Messiah –
  may we never be ashamed to name you.
Gentle and vulnerable God, prepared to suffer for us,
  You show us the painful way of love.
  You are our Saviour –
  May we never be ashamed to name you.   **Amen**

Offering Prayer

Giving God,
you have put into our charge a great treasure –
the truth of your love for us and for the whole world.
Take our gifts, and use them
for the good of all, and for your glory.   **Amen**

Dismissal

God has shown us new things,
hidden things we did not know before;
may we keep safe the treasure put into our charge,
with the help of the Holy Spirit dwelling within us;
And may the grace …

3rd Sunday before Easter
Lent 4

Presentation

*Focus on images of light/darkness. Employ symbolic use of light e.g.
candles at readings, spotlight on cross or flower arrangement. You
can also use mirrors. Teach a modern setting of the Gloria (e.g.
Taizé, Iona).*

Call to Worship

It is not ourselves that we proclaim;
we proclaim Christ Jesus as Lord
and ourselves as your servants for Jesus' sake.

Prayer of Adoration

God of glory,
In the darkness of chaos, before the world began,
   you said 'Let there be light'
   and light shone out, revealing order, bringing hope.
In the darkness of thunder clouds, on a mountain top,
   you spoke to Moses of law and liberation
   and your glory fired the people with hope.
In the darkness of a stable, in an obscure village,
   a small light flickered
   as a baby was born, God with us, bringing hope.
In the darkness of an occupied land,
   you showed Jesus in a new light
   and his friends were dazzled by hope beyond hope.
In the darkness of this passing age,
   a light dawns in our hearts:
   the gospel of the glory of Christ, giving us hope.   **Amen**

Prayer of Petition

I lift my eyes to the hills – from where will help come?
The clouds hang low along the crags.
reminding me of my distress and doubt.
I lift my eyes to the hills – from where will help come?

Like people wandering in the wilderness
we wonder which way to turn.
I lift my eyes to the hills – from where will help come?
Faith is a hard journey, toiling upward
on a narrow path, following but full of questions:
I lift my eyes to the hills – from where will help come?
When your light breaks through the cloud
and we see your glory in the high places,
Lord, help us not to be afraid;
help us to overcome the desire
to enshrine you and stay there on the mountain top;
help us to listen to your voice; and to follow the stony path
back down the mountain into the everyday world.
Our help comes only from you. **Amen**

Prayer of Intercession

God of glory, we remember those who find it hard to see your
light, who are 'blinded by the god of this passing age', distracted
by consumer goods and power games ... We pray that we may, in
our own lives, declare different values, and explore the way of the
gospel.
L: God, in your mercy you have given us this ministry:
R: **May we never lose heart.**
God of glory, we remember those who find it hard to see your
light, who are caught up in situations they cannot control, in wars,
accidents, natural disasters ... may we give practical help where we
can, pray with understanding, and never cease caring.
L: God, in your mercy you have given us this ministry:
R: **May we never lose heart.**
God of glory, we remember those who find it hard to see your
light, who are distressed, lost, depressed, in pain; may we be there
when they need us, to listen to share their pain, and to find words
for what we have experienced: the light of your glory seen in the
face of Jesus.
L: God, in your mercy you have given us this ministry:
R: **May we never lose heart. Amen**

Dismissal

Go into the world, to share the knowledge of God's glory, shining
in the face of Jesus Christ, through the fire of the Holy Spirit
burning in your hearts. **Amen**

Mothering Sunday

Presentation

Members of the congregation could talk about the different kinds of relationships they have. Different cultures would provide new insights.

Call to Worship

Looking around at those who were sitting in a circle about him, Jesus said, 'Here are my mother and my brothers. Whoever does the will of God is my brother and sister and mother.'

Prayer of Adoration

(*Could be linked to Hymns and Psalms 13 v.3 and 16 v.3*)

Loving God, you care for us
at every moment in our lives:
like a mother, like a father, giving life, giving birth;
with us from the beginning:
cradling and feeding, watching and carrying,
walking alongside our first steps,
listening to our first faltering words,
knowing our fears, drying our tears.
You care for each one of us –
all your children, all humanity –
through our growing in grace, our hunger, our hope,
our discoveries and our rebellions.
When we ask for bread, you do not give us a stone;
when we are lost, you find us;
when we leave home, and come back penniless,
you run to welcome and embrace us.
You never give up on your children, all our lives long;
and we praise you, loving God.   **Amen**

Prayer of Confession

Loving God, you have put us in families and communities that we might learn more about you. Forgive us when we have been selfish, arrogant or unkind.

Loving God, Jesus said that those who do your will are his family.
Forgive us when we have been cowardly, lazy or brash.
As we ask forgiveness for the past, we also ask that you will
deepen our faith, strengthen our commitment, and bring us into a
closer relationship with you.
L: God hears our prayers and forgives our sins:
R: **Thanks be to God**.

Prayer of Intercession

Loving God, you call us to faithful obedience and praise.

We pray for those who share your word with us: our ministers,
preachers and teachers.
May they so listen and speak that we may all grow in your wisdom.

We pray for those who generously share the resources you
have given them: time and talent, money and energy.
May we ourselves so give and receive that others may grow in
generosity.

We pray for those who share themselves, placing their trust in us.
May we all so honour each other that we may grow in faith and
self-respect.   **Amen**

Offering Prayer   *Read I Thess. 2.8*

O generous God, as we deepen our devotion to you, our
commitment to each other, our dedication to service in the world,
make us willing to share all that we have, all that we are, for the
building of your kingdom and the glory of your name, this day and
forever.   **Amen**

Dismissal

May the yearning of God
    surround you in your difficulties, enfold you in your sorrows,
    carry you through all dangers, sustain you in all joy
    and bring you safe to glory ...

Lam. 3.18–33
Rom. 5.1–11
Mark 10.32–45

2nd Sunday before Easter
Lent 5   Passion Sunday

Presentation

The Gospel passage would lend itself to a dramatic reading, with four voices (Narrator, Jesus, James, John) and with the congregation invited to identify with the ten other disciples.

Call to Worship

The Lord's love is surely not exhausted, nor has his compassion failed, they are new every morning, so great is his constancy.

Prayer of Adoration

    L: Lord, you are all that we have:
    R: **Therefore we wait for you patiently.**
Your love was there from the beginning:
you looked on all you had created.
including humanity, and saw that it was good.
    L: Lord, you are all that we have:
    R: **Therefore we wait for you patiently.**
You called your people to follow you in faith,
you rescued them from captivity,
you led them in the wilderness,
you fed them in their hunger and rebuked them in their greed,
you spoke to them through the prophets,
you comforted them in exile.
you sang in them a new song.
    L: Lord, you are all that we have:
    R: **Therefore we wait for you patiently.**
You came to us in Jesus,
you called us to be disciples,
you healed the sick and found the lost,
you fed people who were hungry,
you challenged those in power,
you led the way, on the road to suffering and death,
you showed us how to serve.
    L: Lord, you are all that we have:
    R. **Therefore we wait for you patiently.**

You gave your life, a ransom for all humanity
and you rose again,
so that we can see that good overcomes evil,
that even death cannot destroy your love.
   L: Lord, you are all that we have:
   R: **Therefore we wait for you patiently.**

℣ Prayer of Confession

Teacher, how often you have spoken to us
and we have failed to hear
what you were really saying.
How often we have focussed on status or wealth,
material goods or success in worldly terms
as the things that matter, and ignored the secret signs,
the upside-down values of the kingdom.
How often, feeling ourselves of no worth,
we have given way to despair
and, overwhelmed by our failures,
have not had faith in your compassion
and unfailing love.
Forgive us for our failure to listen,
our false hopes, our lack of faith. *Silence*

Christ died for us while we were yet sinners
and that is God's proof of his love towards us.
We exult in God, through our Lord Jesus,
through whom we have now been granted reconciliation. **Amen**

Dismissal

May God, who forgives, give you faith in your new beginnings.
May Jesus, who came to suffer and serve, show you the way.
May the Spirit, who is with us now, enable you to live in
hope. **Amen**

Sunday before Easter
Lent 6   Palm Sunday

Presentation

*Traditions (open air processions/ reading the Passion narrative) are
important. If possible leave space for reflection, amid activity and
words. Focus not just on biblical scene, but on situations now which
cry out Hosanna – come, save.*

Call to Worship

Take to heart among yourselves what you find in Christ Jesus:
welcomed and rejected in his life and death,
as he bore our human likeness and shared our human lot.
Take to heart among yourselves what you find in Christ Jesus.

Prayer of Adoration

Great God,
whose name, mysterious and intimate, is 'I am',
we wonder at your power,
creative and all-encompassing,
and we worship you.

Jesus, Lord of life,
whose name was shouted on the streets
with cries of 'Hosanna' and of 'Crucify',
we wonder at your power,
redemptive and all-encompassing,
and we worship God in you.

Holy Spirit,
perceived in many forms and known by many names,
you dance like flame,
breathe like the wind,
descend like a dove.
As we worship, warm our hearts,
deepen our commitment and prompt our prayers.
In our daily discipleship, be to us
counsellor and advocate, encourager and friend,
for Christ's sake.   **Amen**

Offering Prayer

O God our Saviour and our Servant, we welcome you into our
midst – not with cloaks strewn on the road or palm branches, or
shouts – but with these gifts. May they and we be used in your
service. **Amen**

Prayers of Intercession

We pray for a world that is weary of inequality, poverty and war ...
   L: Blessed is the one who comes in the name of the Lord:
   R: Come save us now – Hosanna.
We pray for those who suffer from prejudice, injustice, abuse,
and those who inflict that suffering ...
   L: Blessed is the one who comes in the name of the Lord:
   R: Come save us now – Hosanna.
We pray for those in power and in the public eye who hear
themselves praised, who are lifted up by the crowd and yet bear
their own frailty – and ours ...
   L: Blessed is the one who comes in the name of the Lord:
   R: Come save us now – Hosanna.
We pray for ourselves: for a response worthy of our Lord and
Teacher,
for feet to follow on the road, for hearing sharp every morning,
to learn what we need to do, for tongues to console the weary with
a timely word,
for hands to serve him and the needs of the world.
   L: Blessed is the one who comes in the name of the Lord:
   R: Come save us now – Hosanna.

Dismissal

Go now, with the help of the Father,
with the encouragement of the Holy Spirit,
in the name of Jesus,
to bind the wounds of the world
with the threefold love of God. **Amen**

Easter Day

Isa. 42.10–16
I Cor. 15.1–11
John 20.1–18

Presentation

*Celebration is the work of the whole people of God: the Beginners'
Easter Garden, flower arrangements, preparation for Communion, a
banner, organ voluntary, new songs, dramatizing (or dancing) the
Gospel. Use all the gifts of your congregation.*

Call to worship

L: The Lord is risen: R: **He is risen indeed: Alleluia!**

Prayer of Adoration

To you we sing a new song: Alleluia: **Alleluia!**
With the whole created world we sing: Alleluia: **Alleluia!**
With sea and land, trees and living creatures,
in the great silence of the mountains
and in the bustle of the city streets: Alleluia: **Alleluia!**
For the world is a wilderness without your love;
we are lost in the darkness without your light;
there is only a chaos of noise without your Word;
we ache with your absence – the emptiness is unbearable –
how can we sing: Alleluia: **Alleluia?**
Yet in the darkness before dawn
a blackbird begins to sing: Alleluia: **Alleluia!**
In the shadows and uncertainty of the garden
hearts beat again with a fresh hope: Alleluia: **Alleluia!**
In the emptiness of the tomb, among its echoes,
there is a voice that reminds us of the living Word: Alleluia:
Alleluia!
Living Lord, to you we sing a new song: Alleluia: **Alleluia!**

Prayer of Confession

Paul said '*I am the least of the apostles, indeed, not fit to be called
an apostle.*'
Merciful God, you see us here, gathered for worship,
offering to be sent out, for the sake of the world – today's apostles.
You see us, you know us through and through, you know
how unworthy we are, how feeble our faith, how strange our

actions.
We do not persecute your church, like Saul,
but we can destroy it in other ways: by apathy,
by bitterness and wrangling, by cosiness, by trying to exclude others,
by narrow interpretations of your Word, by unwillingness to change.
Merciful God, forgive us.
Surprise us, as you did Saul:
turn us round by your power, change us through your love,
and send us out in your grace to share with others,
like Paul and all your unworthy apostles, the resurrection hope.
Amen

Offering Prayer

Living Lord, as the women came early in the morning,
carrying spices to honour your body,
we bring these gifts;
as the men ran, empty handed, to find an empty tomb,
we bring our need;
accept what we offer and bless what we receive in this worship,
that all may be shared to the glory of your name.   **Amen**

Prayer of Intercession   *If possible use a Taizé chant as response.*

We pray for those who mourn ...
– for those who see but do not understand ...
– for those who are anxious and afraid ...
– for those who are beginning to believe ...
– for those for whom resurrection is a fragile hope ...
– for those who want to cling on to the past ...
– for those who are share the good news, in the face of doubt, scorn and apathy ...
And we pray with those who rejoice, who know your resurrection hope ...

Dismissal

Loving Lord, in the dark of the night we fear we have lost you,
on the edge of a new day we feel your presence.
May we hear you call us by name and go out into the world,
to share your good news, in the light of your love.   **Amen**

1st Sunday after Easter

Presentation

*'Seeing' – maybe a collage of the 'visual aid' of grapes (OT lesson),
or the visual/ tactile image of the clay pot (Epistle); explore the
challenge of resurrection for all disciple and the possibility of
declaring 'My Lord and my God'.*

Call to Worship

We, in the spirit of faith, believe and therefore speak out …
so that, as the abundant grace of God is shared
by more and more, the greater may be the chorus of
thanksgiving that rises to the glory of God.

Prayer of Adoration

Creator God,
we cannot see you any more than
we can glimpse the wind,
that shepherds the clouds and stirs the trees.
But we see the power and beauty of your creation
and that is enough to prompt our praise.

Caring God,
we cannot always perceive your love
among the pain and suffering of our world.
But we see Jesus, arrested and tried, tortured and killed,
and risen again to prompt our faith in your love and mercy.

Inspiring God,
we often find it difficult to discern your work
from the outward appearance of your church.
But we recognize that men and women, boys and girls,
are brought to faith and grow in grace,
and that is enough to strengthen our confidence
in your hidden but powerful presence.

Creating, Caring, Inspiring God, help us to acknowledge
that what is seen is here today and gone tomorrow,
but that your love, though unseen, lasts forever.   **Amen**

Meditation

*'Unless I see the mark of the nails on his hand, unless I put my
finger into the place where the nails were, and my hand into his
side, I will never believe ...'*
Unless we meet angels at the empty tomb,
we will go on searching for the living among the dead ...
Unless we have more than the witness of these women,
we will see their story as mere nonsense ...
Unless I know where they have put my Lord's body, I cannot
mourn him ...
Unless he greets us with peace, we will go on being afraid ...
Unless he sits at our table and breaks bread with us,
how can we recognize him? ...
Unless there is room for our questions and doubts,
unless God's humanity meets ours,
unless we see the hope that bears the wounds of the world,
how can we say 'My Lord and my God'?

Prayers of Intercession

For those who are hard-pressed: parents, those with heavy
responsibilities: Peace.
L: May they find faith to say: R: **'My Lord and my God'**.
For those who are bewildered, full of doubts and questions: Peace.
L: May they find faith to say: R: **'My Lord and my God'**.
For those who are hunted: refugees, prisoners of conscience: Peace.
L: May they find faith to say: R: **'My Lord and my God'**.
For those who are struck down, by illness, bereavement,
depression, poverty, unemployment: Peace.
L: May they find faith to say: R: **'My Lord and my God'**.
For ourselves, when we are bewildered, doubting, down: Peace.
L: May we find faith to say: R: **'My Lord and my God'**.
Living Lord, you come to meet us in our moments of despair;
we cannot touch you, but you touch each one of us, different as we
are, in the depths of our being, and you bless us.   **Amen**

Dismissal

With all your doubts, may you still find faith; with all your
imperfections, may Jesus still be revealed in your life;
as you grow older, may you be renewed inwardly; and in good
time, may God raise us all into his presence.   **Amen**

2nd Sunday after Easter

Theme

*Jesus, the Good Shepherd, calls us to love and care for one another,
especially those for whom we have responsibility.*

Call to Worship

The God of all grace called you to eternal glory in Christ.
All power belongs to him for ever and ever!   **Amen**

Prayer of Confession

Lord God, our loving heavenly Father,
we confess our many failures in love.
We have not loved you with the whole of our being;
we have not loved one another
with the selfless love you have shown us in Jesus Christ.
We have closed our eyes to the needs of our neighbours
and have ignored the cries of the needy of the world.
In your loving mercy forgive us and fill us with your love.
In Christ's name we ask it.   **Amen**

God loved the world so much
that he sent his only Son to be the Saviour of the world.
Our sins are forgiven for his sake. Thanks be to God.   **Amen**

Prayer of Thanksgiving

Loving God,
we thank you for the many ways in which you have shown your
love to us.
We thank you for the loving care of our families,
the loving support of our friends
and the loving fellowship of your church.
Most of all we thank you for the love which we have seen
in your Son, Jesus Christ,
for the self-giving love of his life
and his death for us upon the cross.

We thank you that his love conquered sin and death
and that in him we have the promise of eternal life.
Help us to love one another as he loved us.
In his name we ask it.   **Amen**

Prayer of Intercession

Father, we pray to you for the world
which, in love, you have created and redeemed.

We pray for the church throughout the world.
especially for its leaders,
that they may lovingly shepherd the flock
which you have committed to their care.
L: Loving Father: R: **Hear our prayer.**

We pray for the leaders of the nations.
that they may make their decisions with honesty and integrity
and for the good of all.
L: Loving Father: R: **Hear our prayer.**

We pray for those who are in any kind of need or trouble,
but especially we pray for those children
who are denied a loving home and family.
L: Loving Father: R: **Hear our prayer**.

We thank you for all those who have loved us,
especially those who now love you perfectly in heaven.
May we be counted worthy to share with them
the eternal joys of heaven.
These prayers we ask in the name of our Lord and Saviour, Jesus
Christ.   **Amen**

Dismissal

Go out into the world in the love of God
and be a channel of his love to others.

3rd Sunday after Easter

Theme

The Old Testament commands us to love our neighbour as we love ourselves. Jesus commands us to love one another as he has loved us. John shows us that our love for God must be expressed in our love for our fellow-Christians.

Call to Worship

God is love: those who abide in love abide in God, and God abides in them.
Come, let us worship the God who makes his home with us.

Prayer of Approach

Emmanuel, God with us,
though you were in the form of God
you did not cling to equality with God,
but made yourself nothing;
bearing the human likeness, sharing the human lot,
you humbled yourself and were obedient,
even to the point of death, death on a cross.
Therefore God has raised you to the heights
and bestowed on you the name above all names.
So we join with those on earth and in heaven
to praise your glorious name.   **Amen**

Prayer of Confession

Loving Father,
we confess with shame that, because of our laziness and selfishness,
your love has failed to reach others through us.
Sometimes, afraid for our own safety, we have passed by on the other side.
We ask for your forgiveness.
Help us to live as your loving and obedient children;
for Christ's sake.   **Amen**

The Father has sent the son to be the saviour of the world.
Our sins are forgiven for his sake.   **Amen**

Prayer of Intercession

God our Father,
remember in your love the world you have made.

We pray for your church,
that we and all who call themselves Christians
may love one another as Christ has loved us.
Open our eyes to see the needs of those around us
and give us the loving concern to come to their help.
L: Lord, have mercy: R: **Christ, have mercy**.
We pray for those who suffer because hatred and violence have
triumphed over love and forgiveness:
for the bereaved, the injured, the hungry and the homeless,
and for those who care for them.
L: Lord, have mercy: R: **Christ, have mercy**.
We pray for those homes where love has grown cold,
especially for the children torn apart by conflicting loyalties.
L: Lord, have mercy: R: **Christ, have mercy**.
We pray for our own homes and for all whom we love
that we may always be ready to draw others into our family circle.
L: Lord, have mercy: R: **Christ, have mercy**.
We pray for those whom we love but see no longer.
Grant us with them a share in your eternal kingdom.
In Christ's name we ask it.   **Amen**

Dismissal

May the love of the Lord Jesus draw you to himself,
the power of the Lord Jesus strengthen you in his service
and the joy of the Lord Jesus fill your hearts.

4th Sunday after Easter

Theme

God calls us to live in union with Jesus Christ and to show in our lives the fruit of the Spirit. He has chosen us that we might help others to learn that they too are loved by him and that he wants them too to live in union with Jesus Christ.

Call to Worship

Let us worship God,
who has called us out of darkness into his marvellous light.

Prayer of Confession

Holy God,
you have called us to be a holy people.
We confess with shame our pride and self-will.
We have disobeyed your law.
We have gone our own way and done our own thing.
Have mercy on us and forgive us.

The Lord has not treated us as our sins deserve
or repaid us according to our misdeeds.
As far as the east is from the west
so far from us has he put away our offences.
Thanks be to God.   **Amen**

Prayer of Thanksgiving

Almighty Father,
we thank you because you have called us into the fellowship of
your church
and for the love and support that we find among your people.
We thank you for binding us together in the love of Christ
and for giving us a shared task.
Help us always to be obedient to your will.
In Christ's name we ask it.   **Amen**

Prayer of Intercession

Lord God, our loving heavenly Father,
we ask your blessing on your church.
Since you have called us to be holy, help us and all your people
to show in our lives the fruit of your Spirit.
L: Father of mercy: R: **Hear our prayer.**
We ask your blessing on the nations of the world.
Grant to their leaders courage and integrity,
that we may learn to live at peace with one another
and to share the resources of the earth.
L: Father of mercy: R: **Hear our prayer.**
We ask your blessing on those in any kind of need or trouble,
those are ill, whether at home or in hospital,
those who are hungry or homeless
and those who suffer because of the sin of others.
L: Father of mercy: R: **Hear our prayer.**
We remember with thankfulness those who have died
and ask that we, with them, may come to the fulness of eternal joy;
through Jesus Christ our Lord.   **Amen**

Prayer over the Gifts

Almighty God, we offer you our gifts,
and with our gifts we offer ourselves, our souls and bodies,
to be a living sacrifice, holy and acceptable to you;
through Jesus Christ our Lord.   **Amen**

Dismissal

Once you belonged to no one. Now you are God's people.
Go in the strength of his love
to live and work to his praise and glory.

5th Sunday after Easter

Presentation

Whatever we ask in the name of Christ we shall receive. The Holy Spirit teaches us how to pray when we cannot find the right words or our thoughts are too deep to articulate. The story of Abraham teaches us that we should not be afraid to be bold in our requests to God, if our requests are in accordance with his loving purposes. This story could be read in dramatic form.

Call to Worship

Holy Spirit of truth, guide us into all truth
that we may worship the Father in spirit and in truth.

Prayer of Confession

Heavenly Father,
you are always more ready to listen than we are to pray.
We confess our reluctance to ask of you those things
that would enable us to live at peace with you and with ourselves.
Because we are afraid of what you might ask us to do
we have not asked what your will is for us.
When you have not answered our prayers in the way we expected
we thought you were not listening.
Forgive us for our selfishness and pride
and help us to open ourselves once again
to your cleansing and renewing Spirit.
In Christ's name we ask it.　**Amen**

God searches our inmost being and knows our weakness.
He offers us forgiveness and peace.　**Amen**

Prayer of Intercession

Lord God, our loving heavenly Father,
we bring to you our concerns for the church and the world.
We pray for the church:

may we be bold to proclaim the truth of your gospel
in our words and in our deeds.
Give us the courage to fight for justice and peace for all people
everywhere.
L: God of mercy: R: **Hear our prayer.**
We pray for the nations of the world and their leaders:
may they be open to the guidance of your Holy Spirit
that they may lead us to live together in peace and co-operation.
L: God of mercy: R: **Hear our prayer.**
We pray for those who are enslaved by an addiction to drugs or
alcohol;
we pray too for those who profit by their addiction
and those who suffer because of it.
Set them free by the cleansing power of your Holy Spirit.
L: God of mercy: R: **Hear our prayer.**
We pray for those who are ill in mind, body or spirit:
may they know the love and strength of your ever-present Spirit.
L: God of mercy: R: **Hear our prayer.**
We remember with thanksgiving those who have died,
knowing that, through our prayers, we are united with them before
you.
We ask our prayers in the name of our Lord and Saviour, Jesus
Christ.   **Amen**

Prayer over the Gifts

Father,
everything that we have has been given to us by you,
so it is with love and gratitude that we bring these gifts to you.
Take them and use them in your service.
For Christ's sake.   **Amen**

Dismissal

Go out into the world in the power of the Spirit
to proclaim God's love and truth.

6th Sunday after Easter
Sunday after Ascension

Theme

We have been given to Christ to be his body in the world. God, having put all things in subjection beneath the feet of Christ, has given him to the church as head over all things.

Call to Worship

Lord God,
you make the light, you create the darkness;
you are the author of both well-being and woe.
To you belong praise and glory.

Prayer of Approach

Almighty God,
whose mighty strength raised Christ from the dead
and enthroned him at your right hand in heaven,
accept our sacrifice of praise and thanksgiving
which we offer to you through our Lord Jesus Christ,
to whom you have given all government and authority,
power and dominion,
not only in this age but also in the age to come.
In his name we ask it.   **Amen**

Prayer of Thanksgiving

Loving Father,
we thank you for sending your Son to share our human life,
and to die our death upon the cross.
By his death he has destroyed death
and overcome the power of evil.
You raised him from the dead
and now he has returned to the glory of heaven
which was his before the world began.
We thank you for his promise
that he has gone to prepare a place for us,
that one day we too may be where he now is and share his glory.

To you, with the Son and the Holy Spirit,
be all praise and all glory, both now and in all eternity.   **Amen**

Prayer of Intercession

Gracious God,
we pray for the church
that we may be open to the gifts of your grace.
L: Lord, hear us: R: **Christ, hear us.**
We pray for the nations of the world
that your Spirit may lead all people to live in peace.
L: Lord, hear us: R: **Christ, hear us.**
We pray for the members of this congregation,
that our love for one another may be a witness to the love of Christ.
L: Lord, hear us: R: **Christ, hear us.**
We pray for those who live in poverty or distress,
that you will send them help and comfort.
L: Lord, hear us: R: **Christ, hear us.**
We remember the departed,
and pray that we with them may share the joys of heaven.
We ask this through Jesus Christ our Lord.   **Amen**

Prayer over the Gifts

Lord God Almighty, we offer you our gifts,
and with them ourselves,
to be the body of Christ in the world;
for his sake.   **Amen**

Dismissal

All that is Christ's is yours.
Go in his peace and his joy.

Pentecost

Theme

*The promise of God ever present, made to Joshua, and made again
by Jesus to his friends and followers, is fulfilled in the coming of the
Holy Spirit, and makes possible the harvest promised by Jesus.*

Call to Worship

Hear the great things God has done and worship him,
Father, Son and Holy Spirit.

Prayer of Approach

Come, Holy Spirit,
breathe your life into our worship,
that it may be worthy of God's greatness and power.
Set our hearts on fire with love for God
that the worship of our lives may glorify him.
In Christ's name we ask it.   **Amen**

Prayer of Confession

God most holy,
we confess that we have resisted the work of the Holy Spirit in our
lives.
We have not been open to his leading:
we have not been willing to share the good news of Jesus:
we have not wanted to be made holy.
Create in us new hearts, O God,
and renew your Holy Spirit within us.
We ask it in the name of Jesus Christ our Lord.   **Amen**

Everyone who calls on the name of the Lord shall be saved.
Your sins are forgiven. Go in peace.

Prayer of Thanksgiving

Father, Son and Holy Spirit,
Creator, Redeemer and Sanctifier,
we thank you for the world which you have created
and for making us in your image.
When we had marred and defaced that image
you sent the Son to be our Saviour.
When he had returned to the glory that was his from before the
beginning,
you sent the Holy Spirit to be with us for ever.
We thank you because he lives within us to make us holy
and prepare us for the life of heaven.
Father, Son and Holy Spirit,
Creator, Redeemer and Sanctifier,
to you be all praise and glory,
now and for ever.   **Amen**

Prayer of Intercession

Almighty and everlasting God,
send upon your church the power of the Holy Spirit,
that we may fulfil our mission
and show your love and your glory to the world.
Send upon the world the peace of the Holy Spirit,
that people everywhere may learn to live together in unity
and to share fairly the resources of the earth.
Send upon those in any kind of need the comfort of your
Holy Spirit,
that they may know your loving presence with them.
Send upon us the joy of your Holy Spirit,
that we may rejoice with all your saints in heaven,
for whose memory we give you thanks and praise.
These prayers we ask in the name of Jesus Christ
our Lord.   **Amen**

Prayer over the Gifts

Lord God, accept these gifts and use them for your glory;
through Jesus Christ our Lord.   **Amen**

1st Sunday after Pentecost
Trinity Sunday

Deut. 6.4–9
Rom. 8.12–17
Mark 1.9–11

Theme

The words of Deuteronomy remind us of the oneness of God, who reveals himself as Father, Son and Holy Spirit. At the baptism of Jesus, as in the whole of his life, Father, Son and Holy Spirit are seen to be at work. In our lives too the work of Father, Son and Holy Spirit is revealed.

Call to Worship

The Lord our God the Lord is one;
and you must love the Lord your God with all your heart,
and with all your soul and with all your strength.

Prayer of Approach

Father, Son and Holy Spirit, we worship and adore you.
Creator, Redeemer and Sanctifier, we worship and adore you.
God, ever present with your people, we worship and adore you,
now and in all eternity.   **Amen**

Prayer of Confession

Lord God, our loving heavenly Father,
we confess to you that we have not loved you
with all our heart, soul and strength.
We have not loved our neighbours as ourselves.
We have been proud and selfish
and have ignored the needs of our brothers and sisters.
Forgive us for all that is past,
and help us to live in love to one another and to you;
for Christ's sake.   **Amen**

God, whose power is as great as his love, forgives you.
Go in peace.

Prayer of Intercession

Almighty and eternal God,
Jesus has taught us to call you, 'Abba! Father!'
So it is with confidence that we bring to you now
our prayers for the needs of others.

We pray for the church,
that we may pursue truth and justice for all people.
L: Lord, in your mercy: R: **Hear our prayer**.
We pray for the nations of the world,
that we may learn to protect the beauty of creation
and share fairly the resources of the earth.
L: Lord, in your mercy: R: **Hear our prayer**.
We pray for all children, especially those who are orphans
and those who live in unloving homes.
L: Lord, in your mercy: R: **Hear our prayer**.
We remember before you those who now rejoice in your presence
and pray that we may come with them to the fulness of eternal joy.
We ask these prayers in the name of Jesus Christ, your Son, our
Lord.   **Amen**

Prayer over the Gifts

Father, you have given us all things in Christ.
In love and gratitude we offer these gifts to you now.
Accept them for his sake.   **Amen**

Dismissal

Go in peace:
may the love of the Father enfold you,
the wisdom of the Son enlighten you
and the power of the Holy Spirit strengthen you.

2nd Sunday after Pentecost

Theme

God's healing power, seen at work in and through Jesus, is also seen to be at work in and through the church.

Call to Worship

Sovereign Lord,
maker of heaven and earth and sea,
and of everything in them,
we come to worship you.

Prayer of Approach

Almighty God,
we praise you for your power and your glory
which have been revealed in the healing power of Jesus
and in the fearless witness of his friends.
May we also proclaim your power and your glory
not only in our words but in our lives.
In Christ's name we ask it.   **Amen**

Prayer of Confession

God our Father,
we confess that so often we have been fearful in our witness for
Christ.
By our silence we have denied that we are his friends and
followers.
We have been afraid to make new friendships or to offer a helping
hand.
Forgive us for our cowardice
and fill us again with the power of your Spirit;
for Christ's sake.   **Amen**

Jesus Christ came to heal and to save.
In him we have forgiveness of our sins.   **Amen**

Prayer of Intercession

Loving Lord,
we pray for your church;
give us boldness to preach the gospel to all the world
and to bring people of all nations to be the friends and followers of
Jesus.
Guide the leaders of the nations,
that we may be governed in righteousness and peace.
Give to us all the will to use the resources of the earth
to your glory and for the good of all.
Help and comfort those who are lonely and those who mourn;
heal the sick in body, mind or spirit
and provide for the homeless and the hungry.
We remember those who have died in the peace of Christ,
both those who have confessed the faith
and those whose faith is known to you alone.
Grant us with them a share in your eternal kingdom.
We ask it in the name of Jesus Christ, your Son, our Lord.   **Amen**

Prayer over the Gifts

Everything that we have has come to us from you.
With love and gratitude we bring our gifts to you now.
Use them to the glory of your name;
for Christ's sake.   **Amen**

Dismissal

Go out in the power of the Holy Spirit
to proclaim with boldness
the good news of our risen and ascended Lord.

I Sam. 16.14–23
Acts 16.16–24
Mark 5.1–20

3rd Sunday after Pentecost

Presentation

God's healing power, at work through David, is seen supremely in Christ's command of the evil spirits, but is also at work through his friends and followers. The Gospel story could be read dramatically.

Call to Worship

Come, let us sing to the Lord;
let us shout for joy to the Rock of our salvation.
Let us come before God's presence with thanksgiving
and raise a loud shout to the Lord with psalms.

Prayer of Approach

L: We praise you, O God, we acclaim you as Lord:
R: **All creation worships you, the Father everlasting.**
L: To you all angels, all the powers of heaven,
the cherubim and seraphim sing in endless praise:
R: **Holy, holy, holy Lord, God of power and might,
heaven and earth are full of your glory.**

Prayer of Confession

God our loving Father,
we are sorry for the times when we have doubted your power
and fallen into despair.
We have failed to put our trust in you
and lost confidence in your never-failing love.
Remind us that nothing can separate us from your love
and in that certainty help us to face the world with courage.
In Christ's name we ask it.   **Amen**

Merciful Lord,
grant to your faithful people forgiveness and peace,
that we may be made clean from our sin
and serve you with a quiet mind;
through Jesus Christ our Lord.   **Amen**

Prayer of Intercession

Loving Father,
we pray for those who are mentally ill,
whether in hospital or community care,
for those who care for them and for their families.
L: The Lord hears our prayer: R: **Thanks be to God.**
We pray for those who are burdened by depression, anxiety or
guilt,
for those who try to help them and for those who love them.
L: The Lord hears our prayer: R: **Thanks be to God.**
We pray for those who are addicted to drugs, alcohol or gambling,
for those who understand their problem and try to help them
master it,
and for those who suffer with them and because of them.
L: The Lord hears our prayer: R: **Thanks be to God.**
We pray for those who have memories of past hurts which they
cannot forget,
and for those who try to bring them healing.
L: The Lord hears our prayer: R: **Thanks be to God.**
We pray for ourselves that we may learn to leave all our anxieties
with you,
and to trust that, in your good purposes, everything can be made to
work together for our good and your glory.
This we ask in the name of our Lord and Saviour Jesus
Christ.   **Amen**

Prayer over the Gifts

Father, accept these our gifts
and help us to use them wisely and well
that your name may be glorified;
through Jesus Christ our Lord.   **Amen**

Dismissal

Go home to your own people
and tell them what the Lord in his mercy has done for you.

4th Sunday after Pentecost

Theme

Amos was a prophet because God had called and sent him. Paul and Barnabas became missionaries because, through the church in Antioch, God called and sent them. The Twelve undertook their first mission because they were called and sent by Jesus. All mission must be a response to God's calling and sending.

Call to Worship

Let the name of the Lord be blessed
from this time forward for evermore.
From the rising of the sun to its going down
let the name of the Lord be praised.

Prayer of Approach

As we come together to worship you, O God,
open our eyes that we may see your glory,
open our ears that we may hear what you have to say to us,
open our hearts that we may be filled with your love
and open our mouths that we may praise you with joy;
through Jesus Christ our Lord.   **Amen**

Prayer of Confession

Gracious God, we confess with shame our reluctance to obey you.
When you have wanted us to go somewhere we have stayed where we were.
When you wanted us to speak for you we have been silent.
When you have wanted us to reach out in friendship we have turned our backs.
Forgive us for the many ways in which we have grieved you;
in Christ's name we ask it.   **Amen**

Prayer of Thanksgiving

Almighty God,
by the power of your Word
you brought the universe into being from nothing;
by the power of your Holy Spirit
you created life and made us in your image;
when we had marred that image you sent your Son, Jesus Christ,
to remake us in your likeness,
and you sent your Holy Spirit to fill us with love and power
that we might go out into the world in your name
and proclaim the gospel to all people.
With all your people in every time and place
and with all the company of heaven,
we give you thanks and praise;
through Jesus Christ our Lord.   **Amen**

Prayer over the Gifts

Loving Father,
all that we are and all that we have is your gift to us.
With love and joy we offer you our gifts and our prayers
and the whole of our lives, to be used in your service;
for Christ's sake.   **Amen**

Dismissal

Go out into the world with joy and courage
to love and serve the Lord,
rejoicing in the power of the Holy Spirit.

5th Sunday after Pentecost

Presentation

In every generation there are men and women who have forfeited their lives because they have challenged those in authority about their policies or life-style. The story of John or some other martyr can be briefly portrayed.

Call to Worship

The coming of Jesus was heralded by John when he proclaimed a baptism of repentance for the whole people of Israel.

Prayer of Confession

God of faithful Abraham,
we come to say we are sorry
because we have failed to obey your call
to be faithful Christians in the church and the world.
L: Lord hear our prayer: R: **And forgive our sins.**
God of brave King David,
we come to say we are sorry
because we have failed to be courageous
when we have been under pressure to stand up for the right
and to speak up for the truth.
L: Lord hear our prayer: R: **And forgive our sins.**
God and Father of our Lord Jesus Christ,
we come to say we are sorry
because we have failed to be loving
when we knew it was right to be generous and kind.
L: Lord hear our prayer: R: **And forgive our sins.**

Prayer of Thanksgiving and Petition

God our Father, we give you thanks and praise
that you gave Israel a line of kings
culminating in the gift of Jesus Christ,
Son of God and Son of David.
L: O Lord our Redeemer: R: **We give you thanks and praise.**

God our Father, we give you thanks and praise
that you raised up John the Baptist
to point men and women to the coming of Jesus.
We remember how John surrendered his life at Herod's court
in the cause of justice and goodness.
L: O Lord our Redeemer: R: **We give you thanks and praise.**
God our Father, we give you thanks and praise
that you gave your only Son our Saviour Jesus Christ
to suffer death in love for us, on the cross.
We remember how he rose again and prepares a place for us in
heaven.
L: O Lord our Redeemer: R: **We give you thanks and praise.**
God our Father, we give you thanks and praise,
with the faithful men and women of every age
who have surrendered their lives to your service.
Like them may we be transformed by your love
and brought at last to your kingdom in heaven.
L: O Lord our Redeemer: R: **We give you thanks and praise.**

Prayer of Intercession

God of love,
we pray for your church that its leaders and members may
co-operate with all who struggle for peace and justice.
L: Lord in your love: R: **Hear our prayer.**
We pray for all who are frightened, anxious or lonely, at home or
in hospital, and we pray for all who are in prison that may they
receive the care of loving family and friends.
L: Lord in your love: R: **Hear our prayer.**

Blessing

Go in peace and joy with the blessing of God, Father, Son and
Holy Spirit.   **Amen**

6th Sunday after Pentecost

Jer. 23.23–32
Gal. 5.2–11
Mark 8.14–21

Presentation

Every group of believers needs true and faithful teachers and leaders who will keep before them the essentials of good faith and practice. Provide bread with and without yeast, to illustrate the difference!

Call to Worship

God you are true and loving. Nothing can be kept secret from you. You fill both heaven and earth with your presence.

Prayer of Confession

God of pardon and love,
we have placed impossible burdens on others and caused them to fail in the way of faith.
L: Lord have mercy on us: R: **Christ have mercy on us.**
God of pardon and love,
we have preferred our own needs to your honour and glory and have caused others to lose their hope in you.
L: Lord have mercy on us: R: **Christ have mercy on us.**
Lord we have failed to speak of your love and to show it and caused others unnecessary loneliness and suffering.
L: Lord have mercy on us: R: **Christ have mercy on us.**

Prayer of Thanksgiving and Petition

God of all grace,
we praise you,
because you call men and women to be faithful witnesses
to your ways of justice and love.
We give you thanks for the prophets, like Jeremiah,
who promised that you would help us to love in a new way.
We bless you for apostles, like Paul,
who preached the message of the power of the cross.
We bless you for Jesus,
the true bread from heaven, giving life to the world.
With the help of Jesus we dedicate our lives to the way
of justice, to the way of love, to the way of the cross.

Prayers of Intercession

Lord God, in your love for all nations and races,
give to each of them wise and faithful leaders.
L: God of mercy: R: **Protect them with your love.**

Lord God, in your love for Christ's body, the church,
give faithfulness and love
to all pastors and their congregations.
L: God of mercy: R: **Protect them with your love.**

Lord God, in your love for both the strong and the weak,
give to us a concern for all in need
which brings healing to those who are ill
and those who are well.
L: God of mercy: R: **Protect them with your love.**

Offering Prayer

Lord, you have provided us with so much.
Teach us to be generous in all that we give,
in all that we think and in all that we do.

Blessing

Send us out into the world, O God,
with hearts to love you, with wills to serve you
and with lives to proclaim you;
and bless us, each day, with your presence,
Father, Son and Holy Spirit.   **Amen**

7th Sunday after Pentecost

Presentation

We celebrate the ministry of Jesus and others to those who are blind.
Act out the story of the blind man from Bethsaida.

Call to Worship

The great mystery of our religion
is that Christ was made visible in the flesh,
was believed in throughout the world,
and was taken up into glory.

Prayer of Approach

Help us, O God, to enjoy our act of worship today;
to sense the presence of God our Father,
to receive into our hearts the love of Jesus,
and to feel within us the strength of the Holy Spirit.

Prayer of Thanksgiving

Lord in your love and goodness,
you have put us in a universe full of glory
and in a world full of wonder.
L: God of all goodness: R: **We give you our praise**.
Lord in your love and goodness,
you have sent your Son, our Saviour, Jesus Christ
to heal the sick, to give hearing to the deaf,
speech to the dumb and sight to the blind.
L: God of all goodness: R: **We give you our praise**.
Lord in your love and goodness,
you raise up in every generation
men and women who become true friends to those who are blind,
and who show them how to enjoy their life
and develop their skills.
L: God of all goodness: R: **We give you our praise**.

Prayers of Intercession

Lord God,
we read how King Solomon had great wealth.
We pray that today's leaders whose nations have plenty
will share their resources with poorer countries.
L: Lord as we serve others: R: **We are serving you**.

Lord God,
we read how Jesus healed the blind man from Bethsaida.
We pray that our ministry with those who are blind
will always be loving and thoughtful.
L: Lord as we serve others: R: **We are serving you**.

Offering Prayer

Father, across the generations people have brought great treasures
and laid them at the feet of rulers. Today we bring our gifts and
place them before you, the Ruler of all. Accept our gifts and
bless the ways in which we spend our money, for the sake of
Jesus.   **Amen**

Dismissal

Go from God's house,
bearing the love of Christ for all,
sharing the peace of Christ with all
and carrying the gospel of Christ to all.
Receive as you go, the blessing of God,
Father, Son and Holy Spirit.   **Amen**

8th Sunday after Pentecost

Presentation

*Those things which are not possible without faith in God are possible
to those with faith. The story of David and Goliath can be told or
acted out, rather than simply being read as a lesson.*

Call to Worship

Do not let your acceptance of God's grace come to nothing.
Now is the time of God's favour. Now is the day of salvation.

Prayer of Approach

God of all grace,
draw near to us in our prayers with your saving help.
God of all power,
draw near to us in our singing with your healing love.
God of all pity,
draw near to us in our listening with your endless mercy;
through Christ our Lord.   **Amen**

Prayer of Confession

It is to our sorrow and our shame
that we have put obstacles in the way of those
seeking faith in you.
L: Lord have mercy on us: R: **Christ have mercy on us**.
It is to our sorrow and shame
that our lifestyle
has weakened our Christian witness.
L: Lord have mercy on us: R: **Christ have mercy on us**.
It is to our sorrow and shame
that having so many good things
we have shared so little with others.
L: Lord have mercy on us;   R: **Christ have mercy on us**.

Prayer of Thanksgiving

L: For the gift of each day and the rest of each night:
R: **We give thanks to the Lord.**
L: For the love of Jesus and for life in the Spirit:
R: **We give thanks to the Lord.**
L: For the witness of saints and the courage of martyrs:
R: **We give thanks to the Lord.**
L: For the forgiveness of sins and the life of the kingdom:
R: **We give thanks to the Lord.**

Prayer of Intercession

Lord it is your will that the church should be one
and serve you by being loving and just.
L: Lord this we believe: R: **Help our lack of faith.**
Lord it is your will that one day all who are wounded or
handicapped in mind, body or spirit will be made whole.
L: Lord this we believe: R: **Help our lack of faith.**
Lord it is your will that we find in you sufficient grace
for our needs and eternal life in your presence.
L: Lord this we believe: R: **Help our lack of faith.**

Offering Prayer

Heavenly Father,
you accept the praises of the saints and angels in heaven.
Accept also the gratitude with which we bring our gifts
to you now.
May they be part of your loving and healing work; through
Christ our Lord.   **Amen**

Blessing

May the God who is never defeated come to our help;
may the God who never sleeps be our protection;
and may the God who never deserts his people uphold us
now and always.   **Amen**

9th Sunday after Pentecost

Num. 11.24–29
I Cor. 12.14–26
Mark 9.33–41

Presentation

All church members need to be valued by the rest and their gifts and ministries affirmed. Demonstrate, perhaps with a bicycle, the co-ordination of parts of body.

Call to Worship

Though we are many,
we are all baptized into one body
and all have been given to drink of the same Spirit.

Prayer of Approach

To a God who has made us all different:
L: We come with love: R: **We come with praise**.
To a God who has made a world of many colours:
L: We come with love: R: **We come with praise**.
To a God who created a single human race:
L: We come with love: R: **We come with praise**.
To a God who has sent one Saviour for all the world:
L: We come with love: R: **We come with praise**.

Prayer of Confession

God of all grace,
you love the church and call us to care for one another
but we have been careless about each other's feelings.
L: Lord have mercy: R: **Christ have mercy**.
God of all grace,
you love the church and call us to be one together
but we have shown our divisions to the world.
L: Lord have mercy: R: **Christ have mercy**.
God of all grace
you love the church and you call us to rely on each other
but we have been jealous and independent.
L: Lord have mercy: R: **Christ have mercy**.

Prayer of Thanksgiving and Intercession

God our Father,
out of the silence of eternity
you have created the universe and given us this planet:
help us to treasure our resources and share them generously.
L: Lord hear us in your mercy: R: **And answer our prayer.**

God our Father out of the glory of eternity
you gave your Son to die for us and bring us to heaven:
help us to share this good news with all we meet.
L: Lord hear us in your mercy: R: **And answer our prayer.**

God our Father,
out of the joy of eternity
you have poured out your Holy Spirit
on men and women, on the young and the old of every race:
help us to work and pray for justice and peace among nations.
L: Lord hear us in your mercy: R: **And answer our prayer.**

Offering Prayer

Lord, from many backgrounds
we bring to you our gifts and you reject none of them.
With our gifts we offer ourselves to you
to be used for your glory and to be spent in your service;
through Christ our Lord.   **Amen**

10th Sunday after Pentecost

Presentation

It is because God has set his heart on us that he provides us with the commandments. Try a brief drama about a parent's request to a child, which arises out of love.

Opening Prayer

God, we come to worship you in your holiness,
we come to praise you in your love
and we come to adore you in your beauty.
In our worship, our praise and our adoration
help us to enjoy your presence with us
and our time together with each other;
through Christ our Lord.   **Amen**

Prayer of Confession

God our Father,
we know that you love us
but we confess that we have not truly believed it.
We know that your commandments are wise
but we have not kept them.
We know that you give us strength to keep your laws
but we give in to weakness and frailty.
In your mercy we ask you to forgive us,
to pardon our sins
and to set us free to serve you better
and love you more in the days to come.
Through Jesus Christ our Lord.   **Amen**

Prayer of Thanksgiving

Loving God,
we lift up our hearts to you
in gratitude and praise
because, in your love, you have provided us with commandments
by which to live good and holy lives.
We praise you and give you thanks
for sending the prophets to remind us

how good and wise your laws are.
We praise you above all for sending us Jesus your Son
to show us what it means to keep your commandments perfectly.
Help us, every day, to ask for the help of your Holy Spirit
so that we can learn how to love your laws
and receive the strength to obey them;
through Christ our Lord.   **Amen**

Prayers of Intercession

Holy God,
you have called the church to be the instrument of your
loving purposes in the world;
may its love be seen in our mission and outreach.
L: In your love and mercy: R: **Hear our prayer.**

Loving God,
you have called the nations to live in righteousness;
may their leaders pursue the ways of justice and peace.
L: In your love and mercy: R: **Hear our prayer.**

Gracious God,
you draw near with healing strength to all who suffer;
may those who cry out to you in their weakness
find you present with them to meet their needs.
L: In your love and mercy: R: **Hear our prayer.**

Blessing

May God bless us with his peace, Father, Son and Holy
Spirit.   **Amen**

11th Sunday after Pentecost

Presentation

In God's kingdom we must learn to let down our guard and allow God to bring out our true and best selves with one another. Retell quickly in the service Oscar Wilde's story of 'The Selfish Giant'.

Call to Worship

Search me, O God, and know my heart;
test me and know my thoughts.
See if there is any wicked way in me,
and lead me in the way everlasting.

Prayer of Approach

God the Father,
fill our worship with your glory.
God the Son,
bless our worship with your presence.
God the Holy Spirit,
inspire our worship with your gifts.

Prayer of Confession

God of mercy and love,
we come to you with sorrow,
because your church has been busy and trivial
and forgotten how to be loving and straightforward.
God of mercy and love,
we come to you in anger,
because the leaders of the nations
have excused their neglect of simple provisions for the needy.
God of mercy and love,
we come to you in penitence,
because we have failed to be honest and loving
in our dealings with our neighbours and friends.
God of mercy and love,
forgive the sins of the church, heal the sins of the world
and pardon the faults of the sinners who pray to you now.

Prayers of Intercession

Hear us heavenly Father, as we pray for your church.
May it be brave in speaking out against injustice,
courageous in its witness for what is good and true, and
loving in its care for those who are frightened and broken.
L: Lord, hear us: R: **Lord, graciously hear us.**

Hear us, heavenly Father, as we pray for the nations that
they may give priority to good housing, good schooling and
good health care for all.
L: Lord, hear us: R: **Lord, graciously hear us.**

Offering Prayer

Lord, as we bring our gifts to you,
we do not forget our duty to others.
Help us to use all the resources you have given
to your church for the relief of those in need.

Blessing

May the Lord our God bless us with his grace, unite us with his
love and fill us with his peace.   **Amen**

12th Sunday after Pentecost

Presentation

Interview someone who is registered as blind to share with the congregation the ministry they receive from the provision of talking books and talking newspapers.

Call to Worship

The eyes of the blind will be opened, the ears of the deaf unsealed. The lame will leap like a deer and the tongue of the dumb sing for joy.

Prayer of Approach

Lord, open our eyes to see your glory,
open our ears to hear your word,
open our lips to proclaim your praise,
and open our hearts to receive your love.

Prayer of Thanksgiving

Lord of heaven and earth,
in your goodness you have provided us with family, friends and neighbours to love us and care for us.
In your love you have sent your Son Jesus Christ who healed the sick, gave sight to the blind, enabled the lame to walk and the dumb to praise your name.
In your mercy you have raised up men and women through whose love and skill, healing and help still come to those who have little or no sight, and to those who have other forms of disability.
For all the help and skill provided for those in need, we give you thanks and praise.

Prayer of Intercession

Lord,
we remember not only those who are physically blind, but also
those of your children who are spiritually blind.
L: Lord, open our eyes: R: **So we do not miss your purposes**.

Lord,
we remember that, just as we read in biblical times, there are
governments and leaders blind to cruelty, poverty, injustice and
hunger amongst their people.
L: Lord, open our eyes: R: **So we do not miss your purposes**.

Offering Prayer

Lord our God,
though it is your will that none should be handicapped by lack of
sight, hearing or any other disability, troubles such as these come to
men and women, boys and girls.
We pray that the gifts we bring today may be part of the ministry
of this congregation to any whose burdens we can lighten and
whose load we can help to carry.
L: Lord, in your mercy: R: **Hear our prayer**.

Blessing

Lord as we leave this house of prayer and worship send us out with
renewed consecration to your service, with greater reliance on your
saving strength and with a brighter vision of your redeeming
purposes; and may we know your blessing, Father, Son and Holy
Spirit.   **Amen**

13th Sunday after Pentecost

Presentation

*The Lord's people often reject those whom God has sent to them.
Invent a short play showing how a family member rejects good help
offered by other family members.*

Call to Worship

The stone which the builders rejected has become the cornerstone;
this is the Lord's doing, and we marvel at it.

Prayer of Approach

God our Father,
we come to you with hearts that are often cold and ask that you
will warm them with the fire of your love.
We come with minds that are often blind to your will and ask that
you will enlighten them with your wisdom.
We come with lives that are often closed to new things and ask that
you will inspire us with new possibilities.

Prayer of Thanksgiving

Father God,
we give you thanks that you send prophets to the church
and prophets to the nations to call them back to a life of justice and
love.
L: Father we give you thanks: R: **And praise your holy name.**

Father God,
we give you thanks that you gave your Son to be the saviour
of the world and the cornerstone of your plan for our redemption.
L: Father we give you thanks: R: **And praise your holy name.**

Prayer of Intercession

Lord of the church,
we pray that your pastors and people
may hear your word addressed to them in the scriptures
and may be faithful in their exercising of the ministry of
Jesus locally and world-wide.
L: Gracious and holy God: R: **Hear your people's prayers.**

Lord of the nations,
we pray that those who rule
may hear your call to good government
which you speak to their hearts and consciences.
L: Gracious and holy God: R: **Hear your people's prayers.**

Offering Prayer

Lord, help us to respect all who come to us in need.
May we never reject the least of them,
lest we find ourselves rejecting you.
Help us to use these gifts wisely and well
that wounds may be healed, hearts may be warmed
and lives may be made whole.
L: Lord, in your mercy: R: **Hear our prayer.**

Blessing

May the Lord bless us with his grace and fill us with his
peace.   **Amen**

14th Sunday after Pentecost

Presentation

The two great commandments are brought together in the life and death of Jesus himself and in the kingdom of God. Show how as we need two hands, right and left, so we need to keep both commandments.

Call to Worship

To love the Lord with all our heart, with all our understanding and strength and to love our neighbour as ourself is far more important than any burnt offering or sacrifice.

Prayer of Approach

Come Holy Spirit,
giver of life and light;
let your love be in the praise we offer
and in the words that we share
that our worship may bring joy and peace;
through Christ our Lord.   **Amen**

Prayer of Confession

Lord our God,
we confess to you
that we have not loved you with all our heart,
mind, soul and strength;
and that we have not loved our neighbour as ourselves.
Help us to be truly sorry for our sins
and to know in our hearts the joy of your forgiveness,
through Christ our Lord.   **Amen**

Prayer of Thanksgiving

We give you thanks, O God,
that out of the love of Father, Son and Holy Spirit
you have created us to us to love and serve you
and to love and serve each other.
L: God of love: R: **We give you thanks and praise.**

We give you thanks, O God,
that out of the love of Father, Son and Holy Spirit
you have revealed your salvation in Jesus Christ the Lord.
L: God of love: R: **We give you thanks and praise.**

We give you thanks, O God,
that out of the love of Father, Son and Holy Spirit
you help us to be true and loving through gifts of the Spirit.
L: God of love: R: **We give you thanks and praise.**

Prayer of Intercession

Heavenly Father,
you have called the church to be an instrument of your loving
purposes in the world. Teach us to be like Jesus towards everyone
we meet.
Heavenly Father, you call the world to treasure its environment for
future generations. Help leaders and nations to honour you by
looking after the good and beautiful things they see around them.
Heavenly Father,
you call all of us to be a friend to those in need. Help us to notice
others in their troubles and to heal them with our love.
These our prayers we ask you to answer and we pray in the name
of our Lord and Saviour, Jesus Christ.   **Amen**

Dismissal

Go now in peace,
To love the Lord
and serve him in your neighbour.   **Amen**

15th Sunday after Pentecost

Presentation

The links between today's readings are not obvious. Kings tells of an unjust action by the strong against the weak. It would make a good dramatic reading, with parts for Ahab, Jezebel and a narrator.

Call to Worship

Come and worship:
Worship the God of love.
Worship the God of justice.
Worship the God of truth,
to whom be glory and praise. **Amen**

Prayer of Confession

God of all grace,
through Jesus your Son we have heard your command, 'You shall love the Lord your God'. We say that we love you but our lives do not show it. Often we are grudging in the way we give you our time, our abilities and our money.
L: Forgive us: R: **And help us to do better**.
Through Jesus your Son we have heard your command, 'You shall love your neighbour as yourself.' We say that we love other people, but our lives do not show it. Often we behave unlovingly and unjustly.
L: Forgive us: R: **And help us to do better**. *Silence*
May God our Father, and our Lord Jesus Christ who gave himself for our sins, liberate us from all our sinful ways and make us anew in accordance with God's will.

Prayer of Intercession

God of justice,
We pray for powerful people who have influence over the lives of others:
    for those in government who wield political power,
    for those in industry and commerce who have economic power,

for those in the media who have power to shape thought and
action.
We pray for those who are tempted to use their power unjustly, that
they may find wise advisers and learn to act fairly. We pray for
ourselves, that if in any way we have authority over others, we may
learn to act wisely and well.

God of love,
We pray for those whose lives are lacking in love:
   for those caught up in loveless relationships,
   for those who feel they have no one to care for them,
   for those who find it difficult to make friends.
We pray for those whose task is the sharing of love, for carers and
counsellors, for homemakers and pastors. We pray for ourselves,
that we may love one another as you first love us.

God of truth,
We pray for those whose lives are not shaped by your truth:
   for those who have not heard of your coming in Jesus Christ,
   for those who have been taught that you do not exist,
   for those who are in bondage to superstition.
We pray for those whose task it is to explore truth and share it with
others: for scholars and teachers, writers and storytellers, ministers
and preachers.
And we pray for ourselves: that we may know truth as it is in Jesus
and find in it our joy and delight to the end of our lives.   **Amen**

Offering Prayer

Gracious God, in bringing our gifts we bring ourselves.
May we hold nothing back, for you have given us all things in
Christ.   **Amen**

Dismissal

Go now in joy and peace, to walk in the way of the Lord, to
acknowledge him in all you do and know his presence with you,
now and always.   **Amen**

16th Sunday after Pentecost

Presentation

Make a display to illustrate God's generosity to us. Items from the natural world (fruit, flowers etc.) could be supplemented by a Bible and a cross to focus attention on God's greatest gift of all.

Call to Worship

God's love has called us here,
God's presence is promised to us,
God's goodness is all around us,
O come, let us worship!

Prayer of Adoration

God most wonderful,
You are the giver of all things. In the beginning you made the world and all that is in it. In your generous love you have made the human race, to delight in your creation and to know your will. When, in our foolishness, we turned against you, your love knew no limits. You gave us Jesus Christ your Son to be our saviour and our helper. You sent your Holy Spirit to inspire and to empower us. Every day your love surrounds us. From you we have received more than we have asked and more than we deserved. We praise you and we adore you, for you are indeed God most wonderful, ever to be worshipped, world without end.   **Amen**

Meditation

What a terrible waste of money!
All that ointment – and so expensive too!
Just think what could have been done with that money:
    we could have had a new carpet for the vestibule,
    some new toys for the playgroup,
    some new music for the choir,
    some new cups for the kitchen,
    even given something to the poor.

Now we will never have the chance.
It is gone, wasted, poured away in a useless and extravagant
gesture.
Whatever made her do it? Didn't she think about the
consequences?   *Silence*
'She has performed a good service for me.
For you always have the poor with you,
and you can show kindness to them whenever you wish.'   *Silence*
Lord, teach us that love *is* generous, *is* uncalculating, *is*
extravagant. Let our love be like that – our love for you, *and* our
love for the poor alike.

Prayer of Intercession

(*The following is a framework to be filled in with appropriate
topical and local material.*)

We pray for those who are materially poor:
    those who experience drought and famine ...
    those in economically underdeveloped countries ...
    those living on welfare benefits ...
L: Generous God: R: **Help them in their struggles**.

We pray for those who are spiritually poor:
    those who are greedy and grasping ...
    those who care for nobody but themselves ...
    those without any faith in you ...
L: Generous God: R: **Help them in their struggles**.

Offering Prayer

Generous God,
You give us enough for all our needs.
We make our offering gladly and lovingly,
and pray that through it, others may be blessed.   **Amen**

17th Sunday after Pentecost

Presentation

The communion vessels should be placed on the Lord's Table. If the children and young people are not used to being present at communion, make sure they know what the vessels are for. Gather some ideas about what we are doing when we eat our meals together.

Call to Worship   *(Psalm 105.1)*

O give thanks to the Lord, call on his name,
make known his deeds among the people.
Sing to him, sing praises to him;
tell of all his wonderful works.

Prayer of Confession

Lord,
You have invited us to be your friends, gathered round your table
in love, but sometimes we have turned our backs on you and
chosen our own way.
L: We are sorry for all our betrayals: R: **Forgive us, Lord**.
You have promised us your protection in our hour of need, giving
us food for our journey, but sometimes we have been fearful and
doubted you.
L: We are sorry for all our betrayals: R: **Forgive us, Lord**.
You have called us to take up our cross and follow Jesus daily,
promising us blessing as we tread in his footsteps, but sometimes
we have found the sacrifice too great.
L: We are sorry for all our betrayals: R: **Forgive us, Lord**.
Silence
Jesus Christ has taken away sin by the sacrifice of himself.
Through his great love we are forgiven and made free.
Thanks be to God.

Prayer of Thanksgiving

Father we thank you,
   for calling Israel to be your people and for giving her the desire
   to serve you;

for sending Jesus Christ to proclaim the good news and live and
die for the world's salvation;

for giving your Holy Spirit to strengthen those who believe and
to make the things of Jesus real to them;

for calling the church into existence, as a community of faith,
committed to sharing that faith with others;

for nourishing your people with the bread of life as we feed on
bread and wine;

for enriching us with the gift of fellowship as we kneel at the
Lord's Table together;

for leading us out from our worship into the service of other
people, to the glory of your name.

Through Jesus Christ our Lord.   **Amen**

Prayer of Intercession

The Israelites were kept in safety; the Egyptian firstborn died.
Sometimes in this world one person's safety means another's pain.
We pray for

those who suffer at the hands of others,

those who experience loss and bereavement,

those who feel their pain is too great to be borne.

Jesus gathered his disciples round him in the Upper Room, but
Judas went on to betray him.

We pray for

those who feel let down by others,

those who act badly in their relationships,

those who do not feel they belong to any kind of community.

Loving God, in your mercy look upon those in need and by
your presence bind up their wounds and protect them from
harm.   **Amen**

Final Prayer

Lord, you come to us in prayer and song, in silence and speech, in
bread and wine. As we leave this place may we take you with us
wherever we go, so that through our daily living others may know
your peace.   **Amen**

18th Sunday after Pentecost

Presentation

The readings emphasize the need for struggle, wrestling and perseverence in the face of difficulties, before God's will may be known and his presence experienced. This is not an easy idea to communicate. You could ask one of the church musicians to attempt a piece which is just beyond his or her capacity and show how, with struggle and perseverance a performance might be achieved.

Call to Worship (*Col. 1.27*)

Christ is among us, our hope of glory.
Come, let us worship!

Prayer of Confession

L: Lord, when we make our vows of loyalty to you without being prepared for the cost:
R: **Forgive and renew us**.
L: Lord, when we offer ourselves to you in service but fail to sustain our commitment:
R. **Forgive and renew us**.
L: Lord, when we want to know you more deeply but are not willing to wrestle with your truth:
R: **Forgive and renew us**.
Lord, give us your blessing, that with new hope we may receive your forgiveness and be made perfect in Christ.   **Amen**

Prayer of Thanksgiving

Loving Lord,
We thank you for Jesus, who faced the time of his trial and death with courage and trust, knowing that your will was the right way for him.
We thank you for Jacob, who so much wanted to experience your blessing that he wrestled all night.
We thank you for Paul, who went through hardships for the sake of his fellow Christians.

We thank you for all those followers of Jesus, known to us and
unknown, who have persevered in their faith through every
difficulty.
We thank you that you are with us now as you were with them.
Amen

Prayer of Intercession

I ask your prayers for
– those who are searching for God
– those who find the way of Christian discipleship very hard
– those whose faith has led to persecution or suffering.
L: Lord, hear us: R: **Hear us in love.**

I ask your prayers for
– those who have been wounded in life's struggles
– those who who bear the burdens of others
– those who have lost their faith in you.
L: Lord, hear us: R: **Hear us in love.**
Hear us Lord, and grant that through Jesus, the wounded healer, the
world may be healed of its pain.

Prayer of Petition

Help us, gracious God, to love you above all else. When we are
weak, make us strong. When we are seeking, come looking for us.
When we are weary, renew us. When we are faithless, bring us
back to you. Help us never to be discouraged by our problems and
difficulties, but always to find in you the source of our hope and
our deepest joy. Through Jesus Christ our Lord.   **Amen**

Dismissal

May the God of all grace uphold you by his Spirit, that you may be
made perfect in Christ, to the Father's glory.   **Amen**

19th Sunday after Pentecost

Presentation

*The readings are about failure in true discipleship. The Hebrews
passage is very difficult for all-age worship. The story of the golden
calf lends itself to mime or drama, but be careful that the point of the
story comes across.*

Opening Prayer

L: You Lord, are the one true God:
R: **Glory belongs to you alone.**
L: You Lord, are the source of all hope:
R: **Glory belongs to you alone.**
L: You Lord, are worthy of worship:
R: **Glory belongs to you alone.**
L: You Lord, are here in this place:
R: **Glory belongs to you alone.**
In all that we do, in singing and speaking, in silence and listening,
may our love for you grow and our faith be increased. Through
Jesus Christ our Lord.   **Amen**

Prayer of Confession

We have not worshipped golden calves, Lord!
No, but sometimes we have worshipped other things:
  power
  money
  sex
  popularity
  respectability
Silence
We have not betrayed Jesus into the hands of his enemies, Lord!
No, but sometimes we have let him down in other ways:
  selfishness
  greed
  ignorance
  fear
  prejudice
Silence

Lord, we have failed you so often. In your mercy you offer us forgiveness.
Help us to accept it that we may be made anew.   **Amen**

Meditation

Dear God,
I know what it feels like to be betrayed. It hurts a lot when you trust someone and find they have let you down. The promise which was made so readily, but never kept. The confidence which was painful to share, then told to others as if it was no secret at all. The person who, professing to be your friend, said 'You can rely on me', and then proved that you couldn't. The group which, having made you welcome, criticized you behind your back.
These things hurt, Lord, they hurt a lot.
I think of Jesus in Gethsemane. Judas, a friend turned traitor, identified him to his enemies with a kiss. Another friend, as though he had never understood what Jesus believed in, tried to protect him with violence. And all the rest, deserting him and running away.
Were these things even harder to bear than the spear and nails?
When we feel alone, misunderstood and betrayed, we know that Jesus has been there too, and our pain is taken up into his.
Thank you Lord.

Prayer of Intercession

We pray for:
   people who feel betrayed by someone close to them,
   people who feel that nobody understands them,
   people who feel that nobody cares for them.
We pray for:
   people who have no faith in God,
   people who will not let anyone love them,
   people who are bitter and resentful towards others.
L: Lord, in your mercy: **Hear our prayer.**

Dan. 3.13–16
Acts 5.27–42
Mark 14.53–65

20th Sunday after Pentecost

Presentation

The idea that we must sometimes disobey other people in order to obey God is not an easy one to share. Try a mime on the reading from Daniel.

Call to Worship

We come together to hear God's word,
to find God's will,
to obey God's call.
Let us worship God.

Prayer of Confession

Loving God,
In Jesus you have shown us a new way of living.
Forgive us our failure to follow him.
L: Loving God: R: **Forgive us.**
When we have done wrong through fear of others,
worrying about what people might say or think of us.
L: Loving God: R: **Forgive us.**
When we have done wrong through greed and selfishness, wanting
more than our fair share of good things.
L: Loving God: R: **Forgive us.**
When we have done wrong through wanting our own way,
neither listening to others nor caring how they feel.
L: Loving God: R: **Forgive us.**
Loving God, we thank you for the forgiveness which is ours
through Jesus.
May it make us strong and brave to do your will.   **Amen**

Prayer of Thanksgiving and Petition

We thank you, God of truth, for the people in every age who have
been obedient to you even when it cost them much.
We thank you for the story of Shadrach, Meshach and Abednego
who were willing to face the fiery furnace rather than worship false
gods.
We thank you for the story of Peter and the apostles who refused to

stop telling others about Jesus even when powerful people told
them to.
We thank you for Christian people who have borne courageous
witness to their faith, even when they have been made to suffer for
doing so.
Above all, we thank you for Jesus himself, who faced a hostile
crowd, false witnesses, trumped-up charges and even death on the
cross, all for our sakes.
Help us, we pray, to live each day in joyful obedience to your will.
Alert us to the voices which would call us from the path of love
and truth, and strengthen our discipleship, to your praise and glory.
Amen

Prayer of Intercession

God of mercy, we pray for those in need:
  for those who are persecuted for their belief in you;
  for those who live in fear of others;
  for those who are the victims of economic and social injustice;
  for those who feel they do not matter to anyone else;
  for those who have no faith to sustain them in times of difficulty;
  for those who need reassurance of your love at this time.
We ask you to give to these and all your children, your blessing,
your peace, your strength; through Christ our Lord.   **Amen**

Offering Prayer

All that we have comes from you, O Lord.
We bring our gifts in gratitude and obedience, and in praise of your
bounty.   **Amen**

Dismissal

Go in peace and in power.
The Lord whom you serve will be with you always.   **Amen**

21st Sunday after Pentecost

Presentation

The Gospel would make an excellent dramatic reading, with parts for Peter, the servant-girl and a narrator. The younger children could be invited to join in making the noise of a crowing cock at appropriate points.

Call to Worship (*adapted from Psalm 62*)

Trust in God at all times, O people;
pour out your hearts before him;
God is a refuge for us,
steadfast love belongs to the Lord.

Prayer of Thanksgiving

Thank you, heavenly Father, for people with physical courage;
    for those who take action when they see wrong being done,
    for those who protect the weak and the innocent,
    for those who put the safety of others before their own.
Thank you, heavenly Father, for people with spiritual courage:
    for those who speak out against wrong values,
    for those who are not afraid to be known as your friends,
    for those whose hearts are fixed on things of eternal value.
Thank you for the faith which is ours. May we always be loyal to
our Lord in word and deed and serve him in the needs of others.
Amen

Prayer of Intercession

Gracious God, you understand our human weakness and you know
our frailty.
    We pray
– For those of your children whose lives are filled with fear.
    Grant them your presence and your strength.
– For those of your children who know they have let you down.
    Grant them your forgiveness and your peace.

– For those of your children who cannot love themselves.
  Grant them the knowledge that you love them always.
– For those of your children who have lost their way.
  Grant them your guidance and a sense of purpose.
May your love and compassion fill the hearts and lives of the
lonely and the frightened, and may all who call upon you in their
time of need find in you their refuge and their strength.   **Amen**

Prayer of Petition

Loving God,
May your church be strong and courageous, filled with zeal for the
  good news of Jesus and eager to share it with others.
May your church be loving and compassionate, ready to care for
  the weak and to accept those whom society rejects.
May your church be pure and truthful, willing to play her part in
  shaping and serving the world in which you have set her.
May your church be honest and open, admitting her failures and
  seeking to follow you more nearly.
We ask this through Jesus Christ our Lord.   **Amen**

Offering Prayer

Lord,
We have nothing that we can offer you which is not already yours.
As we bring this money we express
    our love for you,
    our commitment to your kingdom,
    our trust in your future for us.
  In the name of Christ our Lord.   **Amen**

Dismissal

L: Go in peace, for God is your refuge:
R: **In the name of Christ.   Amen**

II Sam. 16.1–13
Acts 7.54–8.1
Mark 15.1–21

22nd Sunday after Pentecost

Presentation

*The themes for today, the martyrdom of Stephen and the trial of
Jesus, do not lend themselves to slick presentation, nor should they.
Perhaps members of the congregation, if prepared beforehand,
could recount experiences of rejection or misunderstanding, but this
will need to be handled very carefully.*

Call to Worship

Come,
celebrate the God of justice,
celebrate the God of mercy,
celebrate the God of love.
Together we worship God, Father, Son and Holy Spirit.

Prayer of Confession

L: When our songs of praise are shallow or hollow
   and do not lead to loving deeds, then Lord:
R: **Do not hold this sin against us.**
L: When our loyalties are tested
   and we fail in the test, then Lord:
R: **Do not hold this sin against us.**
L: When we act out of fear of what others may say
   and not out of conviction, then Lord:
R: **Do not hold this sin against us.**
L: When we fail to give to others the tolerance
   we expect from them, then Lord:
R: **Do not hold this sin against us.**
Silence
When our hearts condemn us, God who is greater than our hearts,
and knows all things, grants us his forgiveness and peace.
Thanks be to God.   Amen

Prayer of Intercession

Loving God, we know there is a great difference between the world
as it is, and the world as you want it to be. We bring you our
prayers for those of your children who are victims of the world's
evil. In hope and trust, we pray for:
- those who are made fun of because they are in some way
  different,
- those who feel that everybody else is against them,
- those who cannot forgive others because of what has been
  done to them.

Help them to find hope and a new quality of life.
We pray for:
- those who are persecuted for their beliefs or their race,
- those who are the victims of false accusations and untrue
  stories,
- those who suffer for the wrongdoing of other people.

Help them to find courage and strength to endure.
We pray for:
- those whose lives are filled with bitterness and hate,
- those who find it difficult to trust another person,
- those whose suffering has caused them to lose faith in you.

Help them to find new faith and a sense of purpose.
Loving God, we know that the world is not as you want it to be.
We ask you to use our prayers, and to use us, to help those who
suffer. Through Jesus Christ our Lord.   **Amen**

Meditation

'What have I done to deserve this?' Sometimes we know the
answer. When the innocent suffer – that's when we can hardly bear
it. The baby with an incurable illness, the saintly person confined to
a wheelchair, the child mutilated by a careless driver, the bystander
shot dead in a robbery. What have *they* done to deserve this? That's
what we ask, and there is no answer.
We think of Jesus, standing before Pilate, wrongly accused, beaten
and jeered at, sentenced to death. Then we know that God, our
God, has been there too, and borne it for our sakes.

Dismissal

Go in peace, and find the glory of God in all whom you
meet.   **Amen**

Last Sunday after Pentecost

Theme

Isaiah pictures God's community at a feast which God provides. The beatitudes enshrine the values of God's community, and Revelation shows us the community's ultimate purpose in worship in heaven.

Call to Worship   (*Adapted from Isa. 25.4*)

The Lord God has been
a refuge for the needy,
a shelter from the storm,
a shade from the heat.
We come to worship him.

Prayer of Adoration

O God, great and wonderful,
to you alone belongs glory and honour and power.
You made the whole universe,
everything within it, all that lives and breathes.
In Jesus Christ your Son,
you have shown us what a human life should be like
and called us to follow in his way.
We come to worship and to praise you,
acknowledging that without you we are only half alive
and thanking you for the meaning you give to our lives.
To you, our holy and loving God, be glory, honour and power,
in our worship, in your church and in your world,
now and for ever.   **Amen**

Prayer of Confession

Lord, you have turned our values upside down, and we find it hard
to take.
'Blessed are the poor in spirit', you said;
　but we like to think we are self-sufficient.
'Blessed are the sorrowful', you said;
　but we turn away from sharing the pain of others.

'Blessed are the gentle', you said:
  but we like to get our own way.
'Blessed are those who hunger and thirst for uprightness', you said;
  but we can't be bothered with things like justice.
'Blessed are those who show mercy', you said;
  but we believe in getting our revenge.
'Blessed are the pure in heart', you said;
  but we fill our lives with all kinds of distractions.
'Blessed are the peacemakers', you said;
  but we find peacemaking difficult, and leave it to others.
'Blessed are those who are persecuted in the cause of right', you said;
  but we prefer not to get involved, and to be left alone.
Forgive us, Lord, that we like to take the comfort from our
Christian faith, but too often ignore the challenges it brings us. By
your power, set us free from our failures and help the values of
your kingdom to grow in our hearts and lives, this and every day.
Amen

Offering Prayer

Living Lord,
It is because you give to us generously every day
  that we have these gifts to offer.
As we bring them in thankfulness,
  and offer them in love,
May we grow in the grace of giving,
  now and always.   **Amen**

Dismissal

Go in the peace of God,
  to receive each day as a gift from his hands,
  to live each day by the values of Jesus,
  and to find his Spirit with you in all times and places.
And the blessing of God, Father, Son and Holy Spirit, be with you
always.   **Amen**

Church Anniversary

Presentation

If you can, set out part of the church as if for a party, with people seated on chairs. Leave one chair empty, for whenever we meet for worship there is One unseen who is with us. Gently remind people that he is not the Unseen Guest – he is the Host. Then worship is ready to begin.

Call to Worship   *(Psalm 146. 1–2)*

The Psalmist calls us to worship:
Alleluia!
Praise the Lord, my soul!
I will praise the Lord all my life,
I will make music to my God as long as I live.

Prayer of Confession

God our Father,
This church is precious to us for all sorts of reasons. If we have failed to remember that it is not an end in itself, and if we have made it into an idol,
R: **Hear, forgive and save**.
This church is a place for finding new relationships with you and with one another. If we have broken those relationships, through our failures and our weaknesses,
R: **Hear, forgive and save**.
This church is a place where you welcome everyone to share in your love. If we have made it exclusive, or thought it belonged just to us,
R: **Hear, forgive and save**.
This church is a place where we receive strength to serve others in the name of Jesus. If we have kept the good news to ourselves, or failed to notice the needs of others,
R: **Hear, forgive and save**.   *Silence*
Our gracious God hears our prayer, forgives our sin and sets us free.
R: **Thanks be to God.   Amen**

Meditation

Now and again, in the midst of the ordinary, there is a glimpse of
glory, here in our church:
    a new life, brought for new life, in baptism;
    the faces of children and adults as they return from the
    communion rail;
    the song or hymn that suddenly opens heaven to us;
    the Bible passage which comes alive in our hearts even as it is
    read;
    the love of man and woman shared in marriage vows;
    the moment of solemn hush as we say a final farewell;
    the sudden eruption of spontaneous laughter and sheer joy.
Never quite ours to summon or command – always the gift of our
God who meets us here. Just as when Peter, James and John were
with their friend Jesus on a mountain and saw his glory for just a
moment.
Lord, help us to take those precious moments as your gift to us. By
them, may we be drawn closer to your presence and strengthened
in faith.

Collect

Lord, you have raised up the church to be Christ's body on earth.
Send your Holy Spirit upon us, that we may live and work to your
praise and glory; through Jesus Christ our Lord. **Amen**

Offering Prayer

God,
We would give, not just out of duty or habit, not just because the
church needs the money, but gladly and willingly and lovingly. So
as we offer this money, grant us the grace of being cheerful givers.
Through Jesus Christ our Lord. **Amen**

Dismissal

Go with the glory of God in your lives, to serve him in all
you do. **Amen**

Harvest Festival

Presentation

Three very different kinds of communication could be presented as such: readings from a manual of good practice (Old Testament); a letter to friends (Epistle); a children's story or piece of street theatre (Gospel).

Call to Worship   *(Psalm 67)*

Let the peoples praise you, God;
let all the peoples praise you.
The earth has yielded its harvest;
may God, our God, bless us.

Prayer of Confession

Generous God,
you have put us to live in a world where
there is land enough for every family to farm,
food enough for everyone to eat their fill.
But we have failed to share;
we have traded crops for money
before they were ready for harvest;
we have left others poor and hungry.
Forgive us.
Open-handed God,
you sow your Word freely in our world:
it falls among us, and we do not let it grow:
we shrivel it with our apathy;
we let it feed our fears and fantasies:
we lose it amid our busyness
and, as your children and your church,
we fail to bear fruit.
Forgive us.
Loving God, we know that, again and again,
you offer us forgiveness and a chance to grow.
We come with empty and with open hands –
give us the grace to accept your grace.   **Amen**

Prayer of Intercession

We pray for places and people in the news:
for countries where there is drought or famine ...
where people suffer from hunger, hurt or homelessness because of
wars ...
for peacekeepers, politicians and bankers, as they make life and
death decisions.
L: Lord help us: R: **To bear each others' burdens**.
We pray for people not in the news:
for farmers struggling to feed their families;
those who work all hours to make a living; those who yearn for a
job;
those who wait for a word of encouragement; those who hunger for
the gospel.
L: Lord help us: R: **To bear each others' burdens**.
We pray for the church in these situations:
for aid workers and local congregations ...
for agriculturalists and Bible translators;
for outreach programmes and good neighbours.
L: Lord help us: R: **To bear each others' burdens**.
We pray for our own church community:
in our poverty and our plenty; at our growth points and in our times
of loss;
for those who suffer and those who mourn ...
L: Lord help us: R: **To bear each others' burdens**.

Offering Prayer

Generous God, you have met all our needs
in the gift of your son Jesus Christ, who gave his life freely.
We offer these gifts with the prayer that our lives may bear fruit.
Amen

Dismissal

Go into the world –
to bear each others burdens:
grow in the world –
bearing God's Word of hope.

Appendix

Abbreviations

9C etc	=	9th Sunday before Christmas
C	=	Christmas Day
C1 etc	=	1st Sunday after Christmas
Ep1 etc	=	1st Sunday after Epiphany
6E	=	6th Sunday before Easter
Moth.S	=	Mothering Sunday
E	=	Easter Day
E1 etc	=	1st Sunday after Easter
P	=	Pentecost
P1 etc	=	1st Sunday after Pentecost
PLast	=	Last Sunday after Pentecost
Ch.Ann	=	Church Anniversary
HF	=	Harvest Festival

[A] and [B] refer to JLG2 years A and B

For users of other Lectionaries

The following pages contain a biblical index and a theme index. The biblical index covers all the JLG2 Lectionary passages which occur in years A and B. It is hoped that the theme index is sufficiently comprehensive that those who use lectionaries other than JLG2, or indeed no set lectionary at all, will be able to find material suitable for their purpose without too much difficulty.

Index of Biblical Passages

251

Index of Themes

Index of Themes